The Getaway Home

Discovering Your Home Away from Home

The Getaway Home

Dale Mulfinger

with JIM BUCHTA

The Taunton Press

To my architectural mentors,
Ralph Rapson, James Stageberg, and
John Myers, who collectively nurtured
my quest for architecture

Text © 2004 by Dale Mulfinger
Illustrations © 2004 by The Taunton Press, Inc.
Photographs 2004 by: © Grey Crawford (p. i, iii, v top, 3, 5 left, 13 bottom left, pp. 54–61, 84–89, 96–99, 140–147, 158–163); © Ken Gutmaker (pp. 32–37, 76–83, 152–157, 176–183); © Chipper Hatter (p. ii, pp. 108–115, 132–139); © Tom Hopkins (p. 1 center right, 5 right, 7 top, 11 top, pp. 172-175); © Rob Karosis (p. v middle and bottom, 1 top, 4 right, 12, 13 top, pp. 16–23, 46–53, 100–101, 116–131, 164–171); © davidduncanlivingston.com (p. vi, 1 center left and bottom, 7 bottom, pp. 8–9, p. 11 bottom, pp. 62–75, 90–95); © Jason McConathy (p. 4 left, 6, 10, 13 bottom right, pp. 14–15, 24–31, 38–45, 102–107); © Dale Mulfinger (p. 155)

The Taunton Press
Inspiration for hands-on living®

The Taunton Press, Inc., 63 South Main Street, PO Box 5506, Newtown, CT 06470-5506
e-mail: tp@taunton.com

Distributed by Publishers Group West

Editors: Peter Chapman, Marilyn Zelinsky-Syarto
Interior design: David Bullen
Layout: David Bullen, Lori Wendin
Illustrator: Christine Erikson

Library of Congress Cataloging-in-Publication Data
Mulfinger, Dale, 1943-
  The getaway home : discovering your home away from home / Dale Mulfinger, Jim Buchta.
      p. cm.
  Includes index.
  ISBN 1-56158-599-8
  1. Vacation homes--United States. I. Buchta, Jim. II. Title.
  NA7575.M85 2004
  728.7'2'0973--dc22
                        2004009106

Printed in the United States of America
10 9 8 7 6 5 4 3 2 1

The following manufacturers/names appearing in *The Getaway Home* are trademarks:
Galvalume®, Trex®, Timberpeg®

Acknowledgments

I WOULD LIKE TO THANK all of the people at Taunton for shepherding this work through the editorial and artistic process: Carolyn Mandarano, Maria Taylor, Marilyn Zelinsky-Syarto, Peter Chapman, Maureen Graney, Paula Schlosser, and Wendi Mijal. Also, the photographers: David Livingston, Ken Gutmaker, Grey Crawford, Rob Karosis, Jason McConathy, Tom Hopkins, and Chipper Hatter for painting in vivid color the themes and ideas of these many architects . . . and to Jim Buchta for rewriting my drafts into the best of the English language, the likes of which my high school English teacher had hopes for. I am also most grateful to the owners of these beautiful getaways who have graciously shared them with all of us.

Special thanks to my wife, Jan, my avid assistant on innumerable site visits, chief communicator for this computer-illiterate author, and talented chef who nourished Jim Buchta and myself during our many late-night writing sessions.

Contents

Introduction • 2

The Getaway Dream… • 4

ON THE PLAINS AND IN THE HILLS • 14

A Dog Trot in the Woods • 16
Wyoming

Little Hamlet on the Prairie • 24
Montana

A Screened House in Hill Country • 32
Texas

Reclaiming a Farmstead • 38
Montana

A New Camp Compound • 46
Maine

A Villa in the Hills • 54
California

ALONG THE COAST • 62

A Farmhouse by the Sea • 64
Rhode Island

A Shed under the Stars • 70
Nova Scotia

A Plantation on a Waterway • 76
Florida

A Wilderness Perch with Harbor Views • 84
Washington

Simplicity above the Dunes • 90
New York

A Neighborhood with Ocean Views • 96
California

In the Mountains · 100

A Modern Barn on the Mountainside · 102
Colorado

A Cabin with a Story · 108
Virginia

A House in the Sun · 116
New Mexico

Building a Family Legacy · 124
Montana

A Bit of Italy · 132
West Virginia

A Submerged Ski House in the Snow · 140
California

By the Lake · 146

Celebrating the Forces of Nature · 148
Minnesota

A New Porch Cabin · 152
Wisconsin

A Family-Size Lakefront Lodge · 158
Washington

A Simple Design Deep in the Woods · 164
New Hampshire

An Accessible Getaway · 172
Vermont

At Home among the Trees · 176
Michigan

Architects and Designers · 184

Getaway memories stay with you for a lifetime. My own getaway memories were kindled in college when a friend invited me to his family resort on Lake Vermilion in northern Minnesota. My prairie sensibilities were startled and expanded by the intense blue water, rocky shoreline, and tall pine and birch trees. When a serenade of loons awoke me the first morning, I was hooked.

Since that pivotal getaway weekend in Lake Vermilion, I've designed and built my own lakeside getaway. It reflects the things my wife, Jan, and I love, and it bears the imprint of our personalities, as well as those of the couple we share the house with. In between sojourns to the cabin, I've designed many other hideaways for passionate, energetic clients who want their own unique destination where they can experience nature and create magical memories with family and friends. Some of these homes are featured here, along with getaways by many other architects. I hope that the stories behind these homes inspire you to seek your own getaway dream.

The Getaway Dream ...

WHAT IS IT THAT DRAWS US TO A HOME AWAY from home... and keeps us coming back for more? For some, it's the promise of a relaxing vacation; for others, the chance to pursue a favorite outdoor activity; and for all, it's the opportunity to be in a place we love, doing the things we like best, with family and friends close at hand.

Everyone who yearns for a getaway home knows that it will look and feel different from a home in the city or suburbs. Because a getaway is typically built with discretionary income, there can be something liberating about its design. It may be fun and informal. Joy and whimsy aren't just allowed, they're encouraged. As a result, many of the design decisions are influenced by a desire for self-expression in a way that's rarely possible in a home that has to mind its curb appeal and resale value.

Accessible storage and visual display overlap as reminders of favorite pastimes.

A getaway home is the place for self-expression, even down to the smallest detail like a branded insignia on the mailbox.

For casual meals alfresco, kitchens open to comfortable outdoor spaces.

People build getaways where they love the land, and the design is intimately linked to the terrain.

Along with this freedom of expression, there are some common hallmarks that getaway homes share:

- a getaway sits on land chosen for its magnificence, not for its convenience
- a getaway's views are central to the experience of being there
- a getaway is a comfortable place for casual living
- a getaway creates opportunities for magical experiences

Recycling of buildings to meet the needs of
current homeowners as recreation space and
guest quarters connects the land and its lore
with the lives of today.

the Land . . .

A little place out back pulls us into the landscape as we head off for some quiet time.

It begins with the setting. We build our getaways where we do because we love the terrain, be it a craggy coastline or an expanse of rolling grassland, a place to relax or a base for skiing, hiking, or fishing. Hillside, lakeside, and mountain getaways are typically nestled into the landscape so they sit unobtrusively on the land rather than high on a hill. Coastal retreats are the exception, often perched high on the dunes or on a cliff to take in expansive views of the water.

One of the key things about a getaway is that it is "away," and homeowners and their guests may travel many miles to get to these remote houses. Getting there is part of the fun. A long journey heightens a sense of anticipation as the final approach draws near. A curve in the long drive, a boulder transplanted from the woods to the entry, a tease of the view from the front door through to the back of the house...all help signal the pleasures that lie ahead.

Getaway homes are designed so homeowners can fully enjoy the pleasures of the land. The interweaving of indoor and outdoor spaces is critical to their successful design. Porches, verandas, patios, and courtyards all invite outdoor living and connect the inside of a getaway to the outside. Their position must be planned in response to the the topography of the embracing land.

The character of the land is more than just a view. It's sometimes closer to our feet.

Perched high on a rocky outcropping over the water, this remote island getaway captures breathtaking views of the ocean and the mountains beyond.

the View . . .

This is the view from inside the getaway shown on the facing page. Exterior metal shutters can be lowered to protect the wall of windows during rough weather.

If the land is what draws us to a getaway home, more often than not it's the view that makes us want to stay. In some settings, the view presents itself naturally. In others, you have to work a little harder to see it. The way a house is positioned on the land determines how well it captures the view. There are a couple of ways to optimize the views: one is to set the house at an angle, the other is to turn the house upside down.

The view straight out to the horizon isn't always the best view. At an oceanfront getaway, setting the house at an angle allows you to take advantage of two views at once—one out to the horizon, and the other along the shoreline where the water meets the sand. Another reason to angle a building has to do with the path of the sun—different intensities of sunlight affect where windows should be placed.

A floor plan traditionally has living spaces downstairs, bedrooms upstairs. But several of the getaways featured in this book have the public spaces on the second floor, where uninterrupted views can be enjoyed by everyone during the daytime hours.

Indoors connects to outdoors through banks of windows, where a warm fire can be seen against the wet, cool exterior.

Kicking back on a porch taking in fresh air with a friend, sharing fishing tales, or reflecting on grandma's cooking is the sort of simple pleasure that feels just right for a getaway home.

the Place . . .

A getaway is a comfortable place, a casual place. It's not your everyday home, not somewhere you'd expect to see fine china and fancy furniture on display. A getaway is a gathering place where everyone comes to relax, to enjoy each other's company, and to create new memories of shared experience. This communal spirit affects every room in the house, from kitchens to living and dining spaces to sleeping areas.

Getaways tend to have modest kitchens where lots of shared cooking and eating takes place. At the end of the day when activities are over, husking corn or preparing the day's catch turns into a social occasion. Sleeping spaces take many forms in a getaway. Living rooms, porches, and smaller buildings on the property become places where visitors can spend the night, and communal living takes precedence over privacy.

A getaway home is the place for shared experiences, none more memorable than a leisurely meal at the end of an active day.

A special place to read and write, with bookshelves close at hand, can serve as a retreat within a retreat.

Beams salvaged from an old trestle bridge contribute to the magical ambiance of this sleeping loft tucked under the eaves of a cabin in the woods.

the Magic . . .

And, finally, there's the magic. A getaway is a place for living close to nature, where you can see the stars, feel the night air, hear the ocean, and glimpse the local wildlife from a sleeping porch or viewing tower. Getaways fulfill our dreams of simpler times and simpler lives—from living in a log cabin to ending the day with an outdoor shower (or even roughing it in a home without running water).

A getaway is also a place where social pretension gives way to fun and frivolity, and this is often expressed in the home's architectural details. Whether it's a stair railing with a whimsical leaf cutout pattern or a tree trunk holding up a porch, this freedom of choice in the details allows a getaway to take on the owners' personality more than any other home they've ever lived in. It's just one more reason getaway owners can't imagine spending their free time anywhere else than in their home away from home.

Like something out of *Alice in Wonderland,* this enchanting thick-walled passageway winds mysteriously through a southwestern hideaway.

A getaway porch . . . the perfect spot for living close to nature.

Dragonflies are brought indoors as laser cutouts in a railing detail.

PART ONE

On the Plains and in the Hills

On a sprawling

prairie, an

abandoned farm-

house and

forgotten granary,

deserted for

decades,

become a serene,

private getaway.

A Dog Trot in the Woods

This backyard cabin is surrounded by a forest of cottonwoods, aspen, and fir trees with a view of the Grand Teton mountains in the distance.

ONE OF ANNE MULLER'S EARLIEST MEMORIES IS OF BEING IN A rustic log cabin with her grandparents, the glow of a fire flickering on the ceiling. She longed to re-create that experience during the many years she lived in a New York City high-rise apartment building. When she and her husband moved to a house in the foothills of Wyoming, where a mountain range can be seen far off in the distance and Yellowstone Park is just to the south, she had an opportunity to realize her dream.

The Mullers' new home in a western paradise drew a steady stream of overnight visitors, but there was nowhere to put them in their home. Their solution was to build a guest cabin in a semiremote corner of their own backyard.

A small footbridge built in front of the cabin looks like an extension of the porch. Crossing over the frozen creek bed helps create a sense of adventure when approaching the cabin.

Main house

Woods

Footbridge

Path to cabin

Cabin

A Reclaimed Wood Retreat

The path to the guest cabin meanders through the woods beyond the main house and toward a small stand of trees. Behind the trees, the 1,000-sq.-ft. cabin appears to be a historic relic left in the woods. That's an impression the homeowners wanted to evoke. To achieve this feeling with a new structure, architect Mitch Blake designed the cabin using reclaimed Douglas fir timbers from a century-old trestle bridge that once crossed the Great Salt Lake. The heavily worn wood, full of scratches, nail holes, and scars, gives this cabin its authentically aged look.

CREATING A NEW OLD CABIN The cabin's design was influenced by the decision to use reclaimed wood, which was available only in 8-ft.-long by 16-in.-wide beams. But it took creativity and labor to craft the wood with overhanging dovetailed joints, a technique common to cabins in many parts of the country, such as Tennessee and North Carolina. The technique is efficient but uses a complicated process that requires precision. To give the exterior of the cabin a weathered look, a synthetic chinking, made of silica and sand, was rubbed into the joints, making the concrete look old and worn.

Reclaimed wood used to build the small wooden footbridge leading to the house and the front porch also helps make the whole structure look as if it had been there forever. Since the cabin is built near an old creek bed, it (including its porch) is elevated on craggy stone piers to keep it dry. The timber and rough-cut stones, along with the natural brush landscaping, rusted metal porch handrail, and tin lantern porch lights, combine to make the cabin look generations old.

The getaway was a chance for the homeowners to express their love of old things, including the wood incorporated into the construction. Oak beams salvaged from a pickle factory were used to build colonnades in the cabin, and the walls are made of wood rescued from an old trestle bridge.

A set of six square windows on the back of the cabin evokes the look of an old-fashioned Southern dog trot.

Front to Back Dog Trot

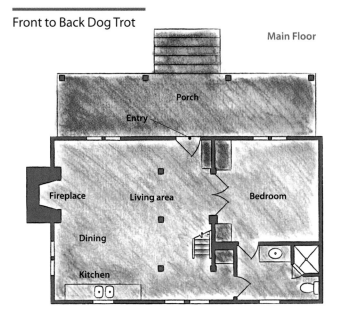

Main Floor

Porch

Entry

Fireplace

Living area

Bedroom

Dining

Kitchen

Loft Plan

Open to below

Loft

An Imaginary Breezeway

The Mullers' getaway is a modified version of the dog-trot cabin, a common rustic style in the Great Smoky Mountains. Traditionally, these houses are built as two little buildings separated by an open dog-trot breezeway but connected by one roof. When designed this way, this cabin was too big to be permitted as a backyard structure (the local limit was 1,000 sq. ft.), so the floor plan was cleverly collapsed.

The compressed layout incorporates the breezeway into the cabin's interior space in the form of a 6-ft.-wide hallway from the front door to the back of the house. On the back wall, opposite the front door, a set of tall windows helps create an illusion of openness. The hallway floor is stone, enhancing the feeling that the space is

IN FOCUS

The loft includes a pair of built-in twin-size beds tucked into the eaves of the cabin's roof. Because the roof is so steep, it is held up by 7-in. by 14-in. purlins and a massive 14-in. by 14-in. ridge beam made from reclaimed timber.

The dog-trot area of the cabin is the hallway between the bedroom and living space. The ladder leads up to the loft.

part of the outdoors. A living room with a vaulted ceiling off to the side of the hallway is made cozy, warm, and inviting by its contrasting wood floor.

Building Traditions

The living room is a special spot where there's often a roaring fire in the big stone fireplace, creating reflections in the frosty windows. It's also a haven close to Anne's heart. For decades, the Mullers have given each other heart-shaped artifacts they've collected during their travels around the world. Not only did the couple discover quite by chance a simple heart carved into the reclaimed wood used to build the cabin, but a carpenter who worked on the project also participated by hiding a few heart-shaped rocks within the structure, including one in the rubble-stone fireplace.

The cabin is never empty, whether the homeowners are there readying it for guests, tending to the fireplace, or chatting with neighbors who stop by for cozy gatherings. The Mullers themselves can't resist staying here together some weekends, making new memories in their own backyard getaway.

The cabin is only a short distance from the main house, but it is hidden in a thicket of trees that helps block views to the house and makes it feel as though it's a world away.

The finishes in the kitchen help the cabin feel as if it were from another era. New cabinets were painted with an antique finish and distressed; countertops of 18-gauge zinc metal sheets were prematurely aged with a slurry of muriatic acid and sawdust.

The cozy bedroom looks out onto the front porch. Salvaged wood doors used here and throughout the retreat add to the timeless character of the cabin.

Little Hamlet on the Prairie

Land around this getaway, long neglected, was revitalized when native grasses were restored and numerous trees and bushes planted.

A ONCE-NEGLECTED PIECE OF LAND WITH A TROUT STREAM AND
a tiny, musty old ranch-hand cabin grew into a vacation enclave for one
family, who come to Montana every year to go fly-fishing, horseback riding,
and hunting. The family started out using the one-room cabin as a temporary shelter while they planned a new home elsewhere on the same property.
But they grew to like the authentic feeling of the structure and decided to add
onto it, turning it into a spacious log cabin. To create even more of a ranch-
like atmosphere as the family's need for space grew, architect Candace
Tillotson-Miller added five outbuildings near the original cabin to complete
the transformation of the forgotten property into a dream hideaway.

A screened porch off the main
cabin, called the field house,
was positioned to offer some
of the best views of the
Montana landscape. The
porch has a dining table and
rocking chairs for ten.

A meandering stone walkway and spacious patio lead to the entry of the main log cabin, which was once a ranch-hand's cabin.

A Rambling Retreat

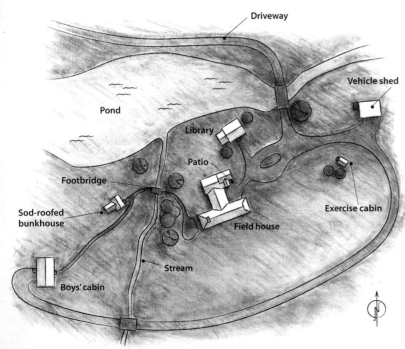

Driveway

Vehicle shed

Pond

Library

Patio

Footbridge

Sod-roofed bunkhouse

Exercise cabin

Field house

Stream

Boys' cabin

A Hidden Enclave

The hideaway is almost invisible from a distance, with weathered wood buildings camouflaged against the parched hillsides. The few clusters of cottonwood trees and low green vegetation offer clues that there's a river off in the distance. Nearest the road, there's a shed used for parking cars, and just beyond that is a small wood bridge over one of the many ponds on the property. Cross over and a group of tiny log buildings comes into view.

The new buildings—the addition on the main field house, an exercise cabin, a library, a sod house, a boys' cabin, and the vehicle shed—all have a weathered, aged-in-place look, partly because they were constructed using rough-hewn wood. Their timeless appearance on the landscape is also due to the modest scale of the structures and the low pitches of the roofs, which match the local architectural style. Since the buildings were carefully designed this way, the group of houses looks like a little hamlet sitting on the land's gentle slopes.

The various styles of front porch on each cabin give the enclave its rich and rustic character. The porches also serve as sturdy places where the family can drop saddles, chaps, or fly creels. Inside each cabin, the rural atmosphere continues—but it is seamlessly blended with the conveniences of a relaxing getaway.

From the dining table, the home-owners can see the Tobacco Root and Ruby Mountains off in the distance. The distinctive ceiling is crafted with lodge poles.

The man-made pond and stream help create a dramatic arrival. The approach road winds through the property, offering glimpses of rustic steel-roofed buildings and horse barns before crossing a small wooden bridge into the center of the enclave.

A Multitude of Gathering Spaces

The interior of the building that became the main field house is not quite the typical little log cabin depicted in the movies. For one, it's hard to tell where the main entrance is: There's a guest bedroom with its own entrance and a protected mudroom entrance for shedding chaps and other equipment. By the time anyone makes it into the main living and social spaces, all the gear is off and there's nothing to do but relax in the great room with its soaring ceiling. The 2,800-sq.-ft. field house has an open plan that is loosely defined by the parallel row of unpeeled wood poles harvested from local forests.

The living/dining room, kitchen, and field house porch used to be the only gathering spots for guests until the homeowners added another cabin, which they call the library. The 600-sq.-ft. one-room building is now a destination to which hosts and guests stroll in the warm evening light. The single room is considered an

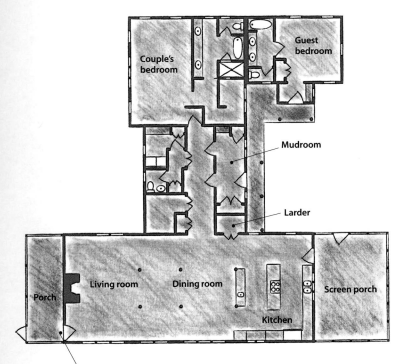

A Finished Field House

Couple's bedroom

Guest bedroom

Mudroom

Larder

Living room

Dining room

Porch

Kitchen

Screen porch

Entryway

COMFORTABLY PREPARED The field house kitchen, reconfigured so several people can comfortably stand around while meals are being prepared, has granite countertops, copper backsplashes, and a center island that also serves as a bar. Like many rural getaways, this Montana ranch is more than an hour from a grocery store, so a well-stocked pantry is important. This house has a 3-ft. by 6-ft. larder (not shown), which has enough rations to supply the family if they get snowed in.

The family's passions for fishing, hunting, and roping cattle require plenty of hooks, shelves, and cubbyholes in the main cabin's mudroom for storing related gear.

The lodge poles that create the dining room ceiling help define the social gathering space. To the left, a bank of windows provides a panoramic view of the foothills.

The library cabin's porch captures views of the Ruby Mountains. Logs used for the porch have visible worm holes and insect-carved grooves. As in a scene from a Western movie, the rocking chairs creak by themselves when the Montana winds blow through the hamlet.

IN FOCUS

Before synthetic insulation was created, sod roofs were traditionally used on buildings in northern locales where temperatures swing wildly. It's a natural way to moderate temperatures inside a dwelling, keeping it cooler in the summer and warmer in the winter. On this farmstead, it's used as a purely whimsical element.

"away" building where anyone can go for privacy. Adding to its charm is a covered porch that is a favored gathering spot for watching sunsets over the hills.

Spreading Out

As more guests began to spend time on the family compound, it became clear that yet another guest space was needed. A sod-roofed cabin built with unpeeled Douglas fir logs was added to the enclave. This one-room cabin, with bathroom and small kitchenette, is accessible by a footbridge over a pond.

Soon after the sod-roofed cabin was built, another structure was designed for the couple's two grown sons. The space, called the "boys' cabin," is a two-bedroom, two-bath structure with its own kitchen, where the two

men live when they visit to tend the horses on the site. The space sits at the back of the property for added privacy, and is accessible by foot or car along a winding driveway. The last structure built, the exercise cabin, is an amenity placed near the other buildings. Though there are numerous buildings that dot the property, the feeling these six buildings create is that of a timeless farmstead, where no single structure is out of scale or sync with the others.

A Screened House in Hill Country

For this family, camping in the backyard means trekking to the screened house down a path behind their main home. Screened walls separate indoors from outdoors in this back-to-nature getaway.

MOST PEOPLE DON'T THINK OF THEIR BACKYARD AS A PRIME vacation spot. But Jim and Coralie Pledger found an ideal retreat right on their own property. When this couple, who live in the hill country of Texas, decided to remodel their permanent home, they needed a place to stay. Rather than live out of a suitcase at a hotel, they asked their architect, William Barbee, if he would also design a structure that the four family members could live in temporarily during the renovation and use later for additional guest space. A screened house was quickly—and affordably—built behind a dense stand of trees on an undeveloped spot on the edge of the family's 2-acre property.

The tiny retreat, tucked behind a stand of trees, can't be seen from the main house. The structure is raised on piers to allow rainwater to filter back into the aquifer recharge zone below.

The Pledgers wanted to treat the land kindly so they built the screened house from eco-friendly products. The material used for the deck and floor is Trex®, a composite lumber made from recycled plastic bags, reclaimed palette wrap, and waste wood.

A rooftop collection system supplies water for an adjacent garden by diverting rainwater from the butterfly-shaped metal roof into a large aboveground metal cistern at the west end of the building.

Tight Quarters

The hideaway is a 1,000-sq.-ft. screened structure designed for year-round indoor and outdoor living. During the 18 months that the Pledgers lived there, they learned that a family doesn't really need much space to get along. They managed to live in harmony during temperature swings of 25° when sometimes the kids had to do their homework with gloves on. In this small space, the Pledgers saw an opportunity to bond with nature—and with each other.

The screened house, a basic rectangular platform, includes one large truss-framed open living area, an efficiency kitchen, a small bath, and two small bedrooms (with insulated walls) that are just large enough for built-in bunk beds and storage cabinets. Since the main house has been completed, the family uses their screened house for overnight guests, neighborhood gatherings, and Girl Scout sleepovers. The space is so versatile it even became a haunted house one Halloween night.

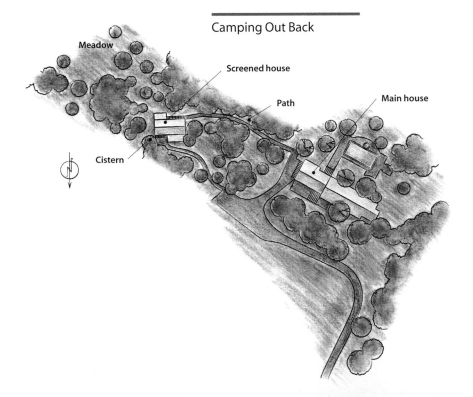

Camping Out Back

Meadow

Screened house

Path

Main house

Cistern

N

The screened house's open floor plan is an adaptable, multifunctional space. The openness of the 500-sq.-ft. combination living, dining, and cooking area means it can accommodate small groups of people or large parties.

Rather than make the end walls solid, the structure is open to the outdoors. Screened walls on each end offer long views out to the property that keep the space from feeling confining. Canvas shades can be rolled down for privacy while retaining warm or cool air, depending on the season. In this open, yet protected, simple screened room in the middle of the woods, homeowners and guests learn to live close to nature.

All-weather, roll-down canvas shades offer protection from wind and rain as well as some privacy.

The interior flooring is a continuation of the Trex decking used outside. The material is almost maintenance free because it doesn't need annual painting or staining, whether it's used indoors or out. It's also warm on the feet in the cooler months and cool to the touch in hot weather.

While the main living area is open to the outdoors, the bunk rooms can be sealed off with sliding barn doors.

A Warm Space

When the Pledgers lived in the screened house, they experienced all the seasons in a year and relied solely on the fireplace for heat in the main living area. The heat generated from the fireplace next to the bedrooms, plus supplemental electric baseboard heat and air-conditioning in the sleeping quarters, helped to regulate the temperatures throughout the year.

This once-temporary structure is now a permanent home away from home right in the Pledgers' backyard. It's a nearby hideaway where they go to camp out when they want to experience fresh air and get a dose of untamed nature without leaving their own suburban neighborhood.

Bedroom built-ins constructed from Alaskan yellow cedar, known for its resistance to weather and insects, and medium-density fiberboard (MDF) were combined to create durable, cost-efficient bunks.

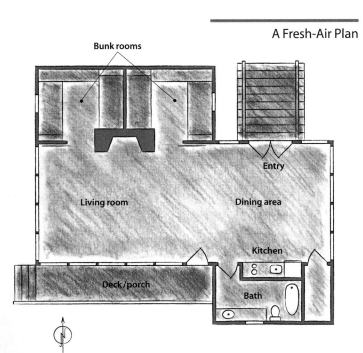

A Fresh-Air Plan

Bunk rooms

Entry

Living room

Dining area

Kitchen

Deck / porch

Bath

N

The front entryway of the screened house leads directly into the kitchen. A pair of torchlights, made from restaurant-grade freezer fixtures and mounted on standard conduit, flank the doorway and light the pathway. The reflective material behind the torches is galvanized metal.

To keep the bedrooms and bathroom warm, each screened opening has a glass window and a galvanized metal shutter that swings up and down for protection from the weather. The modest bathroom offers a pleasing mix of styles with its utilitarian camping sink set in a more elegant granite countertop.

Reclaiming a Farmstead

This once-abandoned farmhouse was given a new lease on life as a rural getaway for a family drawn to the rugged open landscape of Montana. The wood siding and green trim are new but will weather over the years to make the structure look even more comfortable in its environment.

W

ITH A LOT OF ELBOW GREASE AND HELP FROM ARCHITECT

Richard Fernau, a Californian family turned an abandoned old farmhouse

and forgotten granary into a private, serene getaway set on a sprawling

prairie in the foothills of the mountains near Bozeman, Montana. The

buildings, deserted for decades, showed wear and tear as the wild western

weather and local varmints nibbled away at the structures. The surrounding

landscape was so breathtaking that the family decided to take on the chal-

lenge of restoring the interiors of the old farmstead. It took some work, but

the two buildings (plus a new garage) were modernized and moved closer

together to create a compound where the family gathers several times a year.

Three buildings set on acres of prairie stand out against the surrounding mountain backdrop. A new garage and storage shed (far right) join the existing farmhouse (center) and granary (far left).

The entry from the porch leads into a combination living and dining room space. The corner windows in the dining room make the room appear larger by bringing in more light and more of the outdoor view.

The Farmhouse

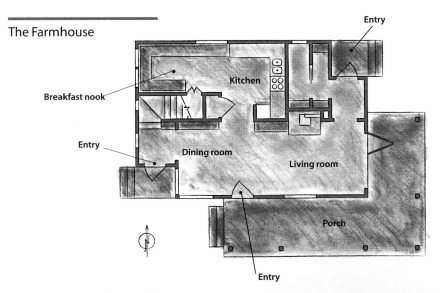

Entry

Kitchen

Breakfast nook

Entry

Dining room

Living room

Porch

Entry

Preserving a **Pioneer** Spirit

The hardy character of the farmstead remains, but the interior has been updated so it's comfortable to stay in for long vacations. From the outside, the buildings look barely touched by an architect's hands. The wood siding on the house is new, but as it weathers over time it will begin to match the original sun-baked siding on the granary building.

The compound feels cozy because the granary was moved 50 yd. closer to the house; it looks as though it's always been in its new location. A new garage blends in with the original buildings, designed to evoke the character of an agrarian building, much like that of an old shed found in the countryside.

The farmhouse, flanked by the granary and the garage, has a new covered porch so the family can sit outside and bask in the mountain views. Bursts of bright color on the doors and window trim, which contrast with the natural wood finish on the rest of the building, are the only other modern touches on the exterior. Inside, the house was gutted and given a more informal, open floor plan to create a brighter interior and better views of the surrounding land.

Old farmhouses typically had a choppy floor plan and small rooms. This reconstructed house blends the old with the new, integrating large new windows with rural interior architecture.

In Focus

The inspiration for the exterior and interior color palette comes from the prairie and all its changing seasonal hues. Window trim is painted sage green, like the lichen found along a nearby stream, and the doors are painted gold, like the color of the summer wheat field. Inside, earthy red walls mimic the dogwood trees in the spring.

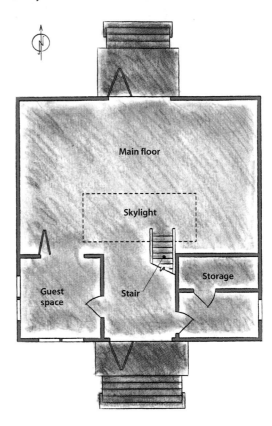

The Granary

Main floor

Skylight

Stair

Guest space

Storage

The upstairs level of the farmhouse is left much as it was in the original floor plan. There are three bedrooms and a ladder in the hallway leading up to a small sleeping loft. The simple shelves in the bedroom have a contemporary feel that helps the small space seem airy.

The feeling of a bygone era in the built-in breakfast nook is enhanced with the plywood canvas and ink-drawn scene depicting the region's history. The sage green walls echo the color of the prairie landscape where cattle graze.

The kitchen and living spaces are open to each other, divided by only a counter. Modern appliances and retro-style light fixtures distinguish the updated kitchen from the old-fashioned atmosphere elsewhere in the house.

The red-stained, wood-sided stairwell is narrow but brightly lit with three wall-mounted lamps. The upstairs hallway is painted a goldenrod tone that matches the color of drying wheat fields.

A Modern Farmhouse Layout

In the old farmhouse floor plan, the kitchen was separated from the living space to isolate the heat and cooking activities. When the interior of the house was gutted and renovated, the kitchen was opened to the rest of the main living spaces to create a flowing, livable floor plan. Sunlight pours into the interior of the 1,200-sq.-ft. farmhouse through the large picture window in the living room.

Upstairs, the floor plan is much like that of the original, with three bedrooms and stairs still in place. A bath was added to the second floor, as was a new roof

Granaries are among the few structures where studs are visible on the outside walls. A layer of wood is installed over the studs inside, creating a smooth surface that makes it easier to fill grain bins. The walls of this granary were refurbished, keeping the farmstead's history intact.

Space to Graze

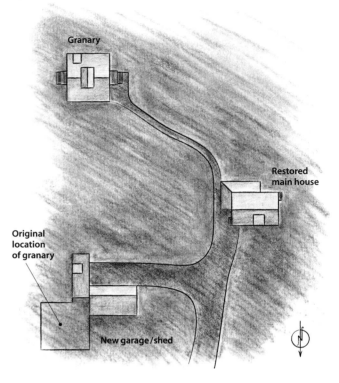

Granary

Restored main house

Original location of granary

New garage/shed

REMODELING AN AGRICULTURAL ICON The exterior of the granary looks old and rustic, while the inside is now a bright, multi-purpose two-level space designed for parties or basketball games. Guests can use a small second-floor bedroom.

The 900-sq.-ft. granary was changed slightly to add more headroom and more natural light by transforming two of the original grain bins into dormers. To bring even light into the gymnasium-like space, the old "head house," where the grain was poured into the granary, was recast as a skylight.

While the newly applied blue-and-green-tinged stain adds a bit of contemporary character to the interior, the character of the old granary wood still reads through.

The glow of new maple floors in the granary beckons vacationers inside for a friendly game of basketball. Even during a vigorous game, players can't miss the relaxing western landscape right outside the door.

dormer, which makes room for a small loft sleeping space for guests.

Although the farmhouse has a compact interior, there's plenty of room for everyone to relax. When the Montana weather isn't conducive to hiking, fly-fishing, or skiing, everyone heads into the granary's gymnasium for a spirited game of basketball. Afterward, the front porch of the farmhouse becomes the favorite spot to watch the snow fall, the leaves change color, or the cattle graze quietly off in the distance.

A New Camp Compound

A campsite nestled in the Maine hills overlooks a nearby lake. Typically, cabin interiors tend to be dark because trees block out the sunlight. Here, double doors with sidelights facing a clearing out to the lake pick up light reflected off the water, brightening the interior.

THE TERM *CAMP* CONJURES A RANGE OF IMAGES, FROM A LONE

woodland hunting cabin before a smoking campfire to a weathered fisher-

man's cottage settled on the shore of a lake to a group of log buildings

nestled deep in a pine-scented forest. This getaway in Maine's hilly terrain

embraces the spirit of these old camps while including a twist or two that

gives the enclave a handcrafted and contemporary look.

Architect Will Winkelman designed a compound of three buildings for a

Canadian couple that embodies the feeling of an old-time Maine campsite. The

new camp sits in a forest clearing on the edge of the lake, with boardwalks,

decks, and terraces connecting the main cabin, a guest house, and a garage.

As you approach the camp along a winding trail, the varied
rooflines make the large getaway seem smaller in scale, giving
it the appearance of a collection of several cabins.

A steep, sheltering roof over a stone terrace establishes the entrance to the main cabin.

A series of wooden hooks on the lakeside of the house is the place to hang up life vests and other gear after a day at the lake.

Rambling Rooms

Traditionally, campsites were built over time in a patch-work way; structures were typically placed on the land at angles so rooms captured views. People avoided cutting down old trees, taking advantage instead of patches of light streaming in between the foliage. This sprawling 5,800-sq.-ft. campsite, including a house flanked by a studio, garage, and guest bunkhouse, was designed to look and feel timeless, as though the additions were added onto the central buildings over the years.

To give this getaway its authentic look, local materials were used. The wood visually connects the buildings to the surrounding forested site. Fieldstone and granite ledge found in dilapidated old stone walls and rundown barn foundations in the area were used to build the fire-place and foundations of the new camp. Roughsawn wood from spruce trees was harvested locally and milled to build the framing of each structure.

The central part of the camp, which the owners call the main camp, is accessible by a covered entry that is marked by a slab of cut stone placed intentionally to blur the transition between indoors and out. It also creates a sheltered spot where family and friends convene early in the morning to enjoy the first sights and

The custom-tailored Douglas fir window frames and triangular glass fit the rounded contours of the stone fireplace.

MAXIMIZING SUNLIGHT While this retreat shares many of the same design characteristics of traditional camps, there's one notable difference that gives this New England–style vacation home its updated look. While older camp buildings could rely on only leaky, single-pane glass for windows, this cabin features large windows of energy-efficient glass.

Big windows fill the cabin interior with light and views to the outdoors. Floor-to-ceiling windows flank the fireplace in the living room. There are windows in unexpected places as well, including the gable ends, which further transform this cabin into a contemporary camp.

One of the cabinets in the main cabin is handcrafted with chunky, rough-hewn birch. The cabinet naturally fits into the setting.

scents of pine trees and to experience the rising sun before heading inside for a hearty breakfast.

Bright Interiors

Long ago, camp dwellers were most concerned about basic shelter and keeping out the cold, so it was common to find cabins with small windows that offered little opportunity for enjoying outdoor views. Nowadays, with the variety of energy-efficient glass available, it's possible to use large picture windows in even the most challenging climates.

The lodge-like living room, with its tall ceilings and massive stone fireplace, brings a hint of traditional camp architecture to the getaway. But the influx of sunlight from an abundance of windows makes this interior

Camp cabins tend to have warrens of rooms. This cabin's open floor plan makes it easier for family members in the kitchen to converse with guests relaxing on the screened porch. The addition of transom windows is another way light is let into the interior—during the winter, the sunlight is reflected off the snow into the cabin interior.

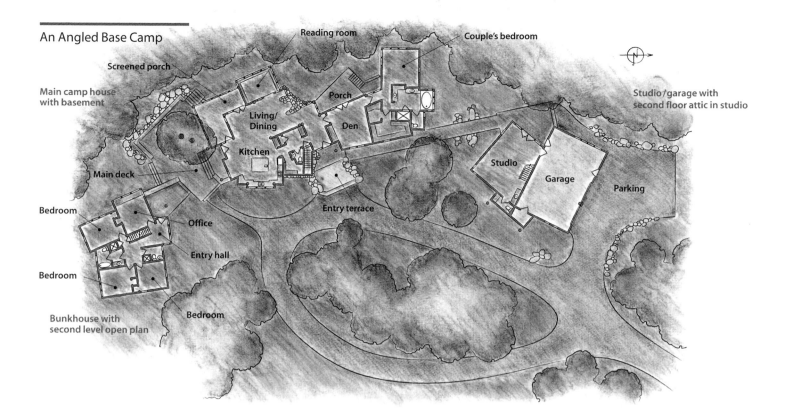

An Angled Base Camp

Reading room

Couple's bedroom

Screened porch

Main camp house with basement

Porch

Studio/garage with second floor attic in studio

Living/Dining

Den

Kitchen

Studio

Garage

Parking

Main deck

Bedroom

Office

Entry terrace

Entry hall

Bedroom

Bedroom

Bunkhouse with second level open plan

IN FOCUS

A hand-peeled birch wishbone king post is more than just decorative; it holds up the roof on this gable end in the main cabin.

Raised decks connect the campsite buildings while allowing the groundwater to drain naturally down to the lake. This deck joins the main cabin to the studio. A bank of operable doors installed at grade level makes it easy to move large objects and projects into and out of the space.

An outdoor mudroom at the entrance to the bunkhouse includes a built-in bench where guests can take off their shoes. The terrace in the foreground between the main cabin and guest cabin is the homeowners' favorite gathering space.

differ from those of olden lodges. Even the wood used—roof trusses of fir and plank wood flooring of light-colored white oak—adds to the brightness of the interior.

Boardwalks Form Outdoor Rooms

A number of wood decks, boardwalks, and stone terraces provide outdoor connections and gathering spaces among the parts of the camp. There's one terrace off the couple's bedroom and another off the studio. The largest terrace, between the main and guest cabins, is a central, multitiered space for relaxing or socializing.

On many mornings, the homeowners can be found on this entryway terrace or on the back deck sipping coffee under the early sun. Come evening, they adjourn to the dock to watch the sun set over the lake.

During the day, the owners can retreat to their private worlds, the husband to an office in the bunkhouse and the wife to her sculpture studio. The 600-sq.-ft. studio is 50 ft. down the boardwalk from the main cabin, just far enough away so the vacationing artist feels as though she's walking off to a private hideaway where she can experiment with her art without interruptions from family members and guests.

Besides the office in the bunkhouse, there are also three bedrooms on the main floor. To complete the guest space, there's an auxiliary kitchen—with green cabinets painted the color of local hemlock trees—so visitors can brew their morning coffee.

The second floor of the bunkhouse is a bedroom for the homeowners' three children and five grandchildren. There's enough separation between the bunkhouse and the main cabin so the kids can raise a ruckus without disturbing anyone else in the camp.

After years of searching, the homeowners found the perfect spot for their retreat in central Maine, a 12-acre parcel of land along an undeveloped lake and a small stream that flows into the lake.

A Villa in the Hills

The shaded dining terrace off the kitchen overlooks the Sonoma hills. The uninterrupted breezes from the hillside that come in through the double doors and open casement windows reduce the need for air-conditioning.

JOHN CANER AND GEORGE BEIER ALWAYS DREAMED OF OWNING

a sun-drenched Tuscan-style vacation home as a retreat from their high-pressure lives as high-tech entrepreneurs. They were able to combine their desire for an exotic oasis with their passion for ecology by using green building techniques and materials to create an environmentally conscious house with European flair up in the Sonoma hills. The house is a cross between a Tuscan villa, with its terra-cotta-tinted stucco walls, and a Sonoma farmhouse, with its metal roofs and wood construction.

Architects Anni Tilt and David Arkin helped turn the vision into reality. The getaway, named "Tip Top" by the owners, is a trio of buildings surrounding a central courtyard. Its hallmark is a belltower-like guest house that welcomes visitors as they slowly drive up the country road.

The compound seems to flow up the hillside while low-riser concrete steps anchor the building to the land.

The view from the tower's covered third-floor observation deck is picture postcard perfect. Instead of locating a bedroom here, the owners made this treasured spot a shared space, as easily accessible to guests as to homeowners.

The fireplace surround and other decorative elements such as the loggia columns were constructed from rammed earth made of locally mined clay, whereas the structural walls were made with a new sprayed-earth process called PISÉ.

A Hillside Beacon

The guest suite is more than a tower. The tall structure emerges out of the hills and signals to homeowners and guests alike that they can leave behind the hustle and bustle of San Francisco—which is only an hour away from the getaway.

Inside, guests find their room on the main level. A study occupies the second level, and an observation deck with a galvanized metal roof and covered balcony is on the top. John, George, and their guests take in the panoramic views of the Sonoma countryside from this upper-level oasis while letting the stresses of city life fade away.

The guest bedroom in the tower has a sitting area overlooking the central courtyard. The concrete floors are tinted a dark color to absorb and retain heat in winter.

SPRAYED EARTH The structural walls of tinted earth make all three buildings appear to slip into the surrounding landscape. Earth-built buildings are energy efficient because the material stabilizes interior temperatures throughout the year. During the winter months, for example, the material captures the warmth emitted from the radiant-heat concrete floors. The 18-in.-thick walls are made with pneumatically impacted stabilized earth (PISÉ), a process in which a carefully controlled mixture of earth, cement, and water is applied through a large, high-pressure hose onto a plywood building form. This new technique is less costly than the more labor-intensive rammed-earth construction.

Minding the Earth

In the great room, high transom windows provide cross-ventilation and help eliminate the need for air-conditioning. When the room gets too hot, heat sensors signal the windows to open automatically.

The placement of the structures follows the contours of the land. Even the getaway's terra-cotta wall color helps the house blend in with the surrounding hills, giving it a timeless look. Each building, including the tower, is constructed with sprayed earth, an insulating material that gives every structure its buff color and helps these ecologically sound buildings stay warm in the winter and cool in the summer. The galvanized metal roofs reflect summer heat off the buildings, another way the interiors stay cool during scorching hot days, reducing the use of air-conditioning.

John and George used recycled materials whenever possible, including fir beams from a decommissioned military building for the framing and cypress boards from old pickle barrels for the ceiling decking. Even the wall insulation was made from fire-retardant newsprint.

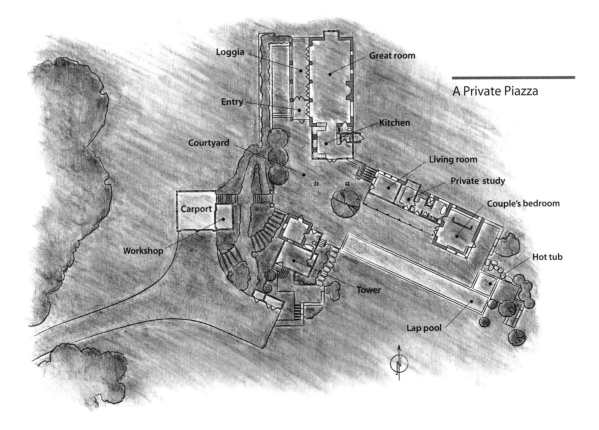

A Private Piazza

Loggia · Great room · Entry · Kitchen · Courtyard · Living room · Private study · Couple's bedroom · Carport · Workshop · Tower · Hot tub · Lap pool

The dining terrace on the courtyard is the central connection between the two main wings of the compound. The tower is accessible by the staircase across the way.

The **Hub** of Activity

The tower is one of three separate structures built around a central outdoor courtyard. The style and color of the buildings, as well as the stone flooring and the vivid landscape views, evoke the feeling of a Tuscan piazza. Almost every room has access to the courtyard, which is the heart of this home. Homeowners and guests alike use it to walk from building to building.

One section of the courtyard is covered by a pergola and serves as the dining area. Wherever anyone stands in the courtyard, the kitchen is in plain view. The buildings were located not only to capture John and George's favorite panorama of the Sonoma hills but also to frame the sunset, which they drink in while sipping wine on the courtyard and enjoying the last glimpse of daylight.

IN FOCUS

The homeowners insisted on using reclaimed materials, such as Douglas fir beams, cypress decking, and salvaged doors and windows, where feasible. The cedar wood siding and the old-wood Dutch door blend with the sprayed earth walls and patio to create this earth-friendly, unpretentious entryway.

A great room behind the kitchen is used for parties, but the space near the fireplace has a comforting coziness that draws the couple when they are alone. A loggia, parallel to the great room, faces the hillside, offering privacy from the public piazza where everyone convenes. It's used for secluded dinners and special gatherings.

Adjoining the public wing with the great room and kitchen is a more private wing that includes the couple's bedroom, a study, and a small, private living room. The 200-sq.-ft. bedroom has its own outdoor shower and access to the outdoor lap pool, which runs the length of the building. It's a cherished place where the homeowners can take a nighttime swim while watching the stars dance over the hills.

The comfort of natural breezes, the textures of reclaimed wood, and the blush of earthen walls are just a few of the pleasures an ecologically attuned getaway can offer homeowners and their visitors. This carefully planned house proves that a green building can be a welcoming and comfortable retreat.

A study in the bedroom wing has views through corner windows (right). Getting into the high, built-in window seat in the same room is half the fun. Instead of a ladder, there's a set of toeholds screwed into the wall.

The rooflines of the compound follow the hilly contours of the land. The retreat is tucked into the hillside for maximum privacy.

PART TWO

Along the Coast

FROM INSIDE THEIR

GETAWAY, THEY CAN

SEE THE MOON MOVE

THROUGH THE SKY

AND HEAR, CRYSTAL

CLEAR, THE SOUNDS OF

WHALES BLOWING

IN THE BAY.

A Farmhouse by the Sea

The traditional white-trimmed windows and doors help this new getaway fit in well with the older New England–style farmhouses that dot the island.

H

of pounding surf and a faraway lighthouse bell—resonated so much with

one family during weekend sailing trips to Block Island that they decided to

build a vacation home right there on the coastline.

Their farmhouse, designed by architect James Estes, reflects the island's

vernacular traditions, even down to the old-fashioned screen door that

slams shut from the frequent ocean breezes. Though the simple shingle-

style home blends in with the older houses nearby, there's a unique terrace

that expands the living space of this 1,000-sq.-ft. getaway and lets the home-

owners enjoy the ocean spray even during the cooler months.

The view to the ocean draws the homeowners back to their getaway time after time. Two window walls joined at the corner of the living room make the house feel larger by bringing the diagonal floor-to-ceiling view indoors.

To create the sense of an outdoor room, sliding walls attach to the shed-style roofs of the porch and storage building. When the sliding walls are closed, typically during days when the ocean breeze is strong, the windows enhance the magical, protected feeling of the space.

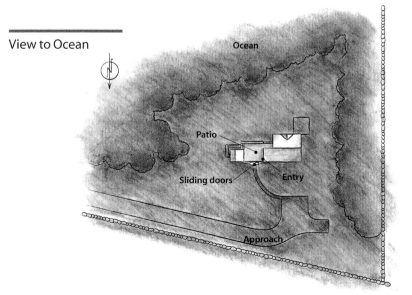

View to Ocean

Ocean

Patio

Sliding doors

Entry

Approach

A Central Terrace

The weathered gray farmhouse is located on a meadow and sits 1,200 ft. from the shore. An outdoor living room built on a stone terrace is visible upon approach to the house. The angle of the terrace is just right, letting the homeowners see the glow of one of the island's historic lighthouses while they experience the ocean views and saltwater spray up close.

The terrace faces out to the water and is sited to frame the ocean view. But the terrace plays an even more important role in the design of this getaway. The main house flanks one side of the terrace, with a small 72-sq.-ft. shed on the other side. The position of the two buildings transforms the terrace into an indoor-outdoor space when two sliding wood walls, complete with two glass windows, come together via an overhead track to form a windbreak. During the summer and fall, this indoor-outdoor space is the heart of the house, the place where homeowners and guests eat and relax while gazing at the ocean.

The sliding walls are what make this outdoor space feel like an indoor room. When shut, they create an 8-ft.-high wall that connects the main house to the storage shed. Even on nights when the north wind whips across the meadow, the homeowners are still able to sit outside taking in the view, protected on three sides with the stars and the sky as their ceiling.

IN FOCUS

Seaside houses need protection from salty air. Here, low-maintenance materials like cedar shingles and galvanized-steel hardware are used inside and out. They take on a weathered patina and help make the house as durable as Block Island's rugged landscape.

The entryway does double duty as a piano niche. Aside from this color accent, most of the walls in the house are clean white to reflect as much light as possible throughout the interior.

A Simple and Compact Floor Plan

From the front, the two-story house looks like any other farmhouse on Block Island. Inside, it has a simple, compact floor plan. The ample living and dining room downstairs, two bedrooms upstairs, small kitchen, and back entryway create an efficient beach house. In addition, no space is wasted on hallways, giving over more square footage to each room.

As in most small getaways, this house has limited storage. That means the homeowners and their guests arrive light on luggage. Just as it ought to be, a stay at this beach house encourages simplicity and an unencumbered lifestyle.

Although the house is small, the windows in each room frame the ocean view, connecting the hideaway to the sights of the sea and the sounds of the rolling surf. The house's simple, neutral materials help the structure visually recede into the meadow. By using the architecture of the house to frame every possible ocean view, the island's salty air, ethereal fog, and sparkle of the sun on the deep blue sea take center stage in this family's getaway experience.

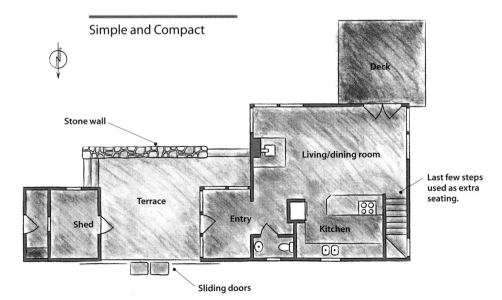

Simple and Compact

Casual and cheery, this living space
demonstrates how moderation
and simplicity can provide all one
needs in a getaway space.

The two upstairs bedrooms
are small and storage is limited, but there's extra space in
the attic, which is accessible
via a ship-style ladder
mounted to the hallway wall.

A Shed under the Stars

The dining area, located in the uninsulated part of the house, overlooks the ocean. The glass walls are protected from high winds and heat loss by exterior metal panels that can be lowered during the roughest weather.

THE WEATHER ON CAPE BRETON IS CONSIDERED TO BE SOME OF
the harshest and most unpredictable in all of North America. But this area
of Canada also has one of the most rugged, beautiful landscapes on the continent. The cape's tempestuous climate and the clarity of the dazzling celes-
tial displays seen here drew Esther, a landscape designer, and Bill Danielson,
a meteorologist, to this place, where they bought a remote ocean-view lot.

After years of summering in temporary shelters on their piece of land,
the Danielsons asked architect Brian MacKay-Lyons to design a more permanent structure that would protect them from the cape's elements while letting them fully experience nature's gifts. As a result, the Danielsons' getaway

**This hideaway sits astride the craggy coastline of Cape
Breton on a remote, undeveloped piece of land six
hours from Halifax, the nearest city. The main house
and the guest cabin were both partially built off site,
trucked into the property, and then assembled.**

A wall plane, made out of corrugated metal (shown closed in this photo), can be raised to expose the window walls into the dining area. The bottom photo on the facing page shows the wall in the up position.

SNAP SHOT

Given their vocations and passions, it's not unusual for the Danielsons to wake up at 4:00 in the morning to photograph the night skies filled with the northern lights. So what could be better than sleeping on an outdoor platform built onto the side of the house? Esther and Bill often grab a sleeping bag, telescope, and camera and head outdoors for a night of nocturnal observations on the 12-ft.-wide wood deck.

is a 1,000-sq.-ft. metal and wood cabin with separate guest quarters perched high above a steep bluff over the roiling ocean and under the star-studded sky.

Connecting Two Worlds

The Danielsons, who live in Boston, make a long trek that culminates in a short ferry ride to Cape Breton, driving hairpin turns over the island's Smokey Mountain, and then heading through a Canadian national park before they catch a glimpse of their getaway in the hilltops. After a few more sharp curves, they park the car and stroll down a stone path onto a boardwalk that leads to the deck where the cabin and guesthouse frame the view of the vast sea.

When Brian met the couple, the architect noted how easily the Danielsons had adapted to living in a series of odd structures, including an 80-sq.-ft. backyard shed they erected on this site. The vision for the getaway became obvious—a shed-style cabin with an additional

guest space that lets the homeowners vacation as close to nature as possible. The buildings, set on a wooden platform that sits on a series of concrete piers, are layered with unusual materials and design features that let the Danielsons adjust their home so it protects them from—or opens them to—the coast's ever-changing weather patterns.

The main cabin, built from galvanized metal and spruce, has the industrial look of a storage shed. The three-sided roof is made of Galvalume® metal panels. Its unique shape has a purpose. One side of the roof bends

A wood walkway provides a clear path to the house and a direct view out to the ocean. The main cabin (left) and the unheated guest space (right) sit on top of 120-ft.-long wood decking secured to the land with concrete piers.

Sliding barn doors open to reveal the galley kitchen in the inner shed. The narrow dinette is placed under a window that receives full sun during summer and winter.

A reading nook built next to the wood stove is arguably the warmest part of the room when it's cold outside. The Danielsons call the nook the "Zen view." It gives the person sitting at the window a framed view to appreciate.

over and sits low on the wall so it can project rainwater down and away from the structure. (Many rural buildings on Cape Breton Island have metal roofs that protect them in just this way.)

The entrance to the main cabin slides open to connect the exterior world with the interior. It's a design that lets the Danielsons live in two partially temperature-controlled environments so they can be as close to nature as the weather permits.

Linear Living

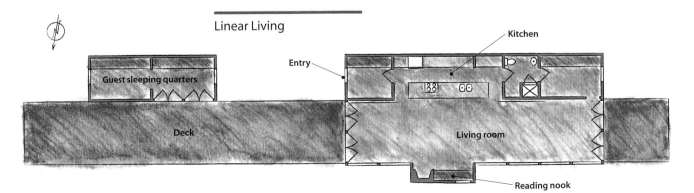

Guest sleeping quarters

Deck

Entry

Kitchen

Living room

Reading nook

In the uninsulated living space of the main house, a loft with a view to the ocean is accessible by a pair of ladders. This is a favorite sleeping spot for the couple's grandchildren. The outdoor deck has been allowed to weather, but the indoor flooring received a coat of protective clear varnish.

Wrapped Inside

The main cabin is a shed within a shed. An insulated interior core (containing kitchen, dining area, bedroom, and bath) is habitable year-round, while an outer shed wraps around the core and is usable only during warmer months.

A set of sliding doors separates the insulated core from the outer shed, and most of the year, the Danielsons keep the doors open. When the temperatures drop below freezing, they close the doors to the outer area and live inside the cozy insulated space.

While the whole house is not protected from the blowing snow and gale-force winds, the couple can stay close to the sounds of the surf, wind, and rain. Even from within the inner shell, they can look out the windows and see the moon move through the sky. There are even times when they hear, crystal-clear, the sounds of whales blowing in the bay.

A Plantation on a Waterway

A deep roof overhang makes the second-story veranda of a contemporary plantation-style getaway, a well-shaded destination for relief from the sun.

W

INTERING ON THE INTERCOASTAL WATERWAY IN FLORIDA OFFERED one family the benefits of living steps away from the sea without the building restrictions that sometimes govern prime oceanfront properties. Nellie DeBruyn steered clear of traditional beachside developments for one that would accommodate her love of bright color and contemporary, open interior spaces. Grayton Beach, a quiet, relaxed development, suits the family perfectly, and they were able to build just the sort of getaway they envisioned far from their home in snowy, cold Minnesota.

The family now vacations in a modern plantation-style home a short walk away from the waters off the Gulf of Mexico. Their community,

The living room is a large, open space under a ceiling of birch plywood. Painted plaster and concrete block give the room a modern look, satisfying the homeowner's desire for an untraditional beach house interior.

The tiled outdoor shower stall has a small window that brings dappled light into an interior shower.

Grayton Beach, has a permissive attitude towards design stemming from its century-old history of hosting eccentric and liberated communities of people.

A Plan for Water Views

Architect Dale Mulfinger was inspired by the old plantation houses of the south, but he wasn't a slave to the style. On the waterfront side of this simple rectangular house, tall pillars evoke the quite elegance of a symmetrical plantation–style façade. But on the street-facing side (see the top right photo on p. 83), bold hues and contemporary lines present a dramatic contrast, complete with recessed bays for the entry and an outdoor shower.

Traditional plantation-house architecture—where the living spaces are located on the second floor to capture the best breezes—informs the layout of Nellie's beach house. Here, a similar inverted floor plan, with

IN FOCUS

Open cabinets make it easier for guests to find their way around the kitchen. The cherry cabinets shown here create a playful geometric pattern against the white plaster wall. Elsewhere in the kitchen, cabinets with frosted glass doors give guests a limited view of the contents while keeping clutter at bay.

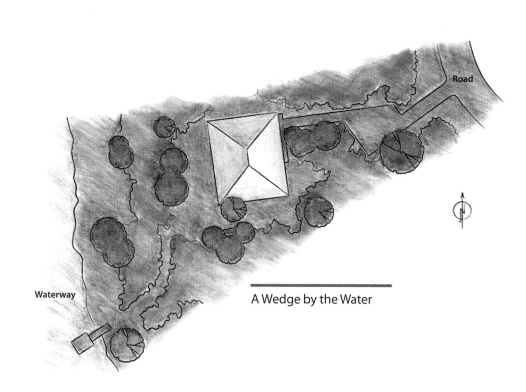

Waterway

A Wedge by the Water

The large picture window and glass doors to the veranda offer extended views from the couple's second-floor bedroom down to the intercoastal waterway. When the doors are open, the home-owners feel as if they are sleeping outdoors.

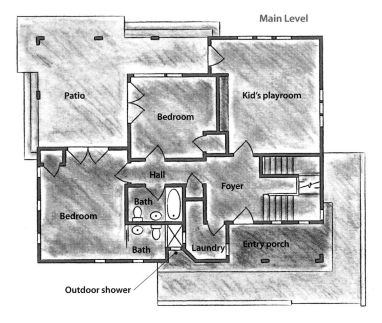

Main Level

Patio

Bedroom

Kid's playroom

Hall

Foyer

Bath

Bedroom

Bath

Laundry

Entry porch

Outdoor shower

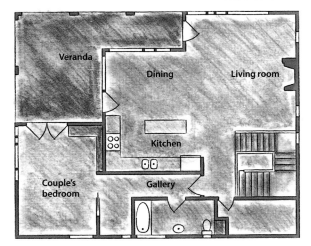

Upper Level

Veranda

Dining

Living room

Kitchen

Couple's
bedroom

Gallery

Terra-cotta stained concrete floors in the entryway and thin, metal railings are contemporary features that give the beach house its inventive spirit.

living room, kitchen, and dining area on the second floor, gives the homeowners prime views of the water and occasional glimpses of the pleasure boats that meander by.

The Color of Sunsets

On warm nights, the room that gets used most is the second-floor veranda tucked into a corner of the house, which affords clear views of the setting sun. But when everyone comes together indoors for nighttime conversation, they invariably gather around the orange and yellow plaster fireplace in the living room. The red flames against the warm colors of the fireplace surround mimic

Preparing food is not a top priority in this beach house, so the kitchen is compact. There are enough cabinets to store the basics, but the house is close to town, making it easy to replenish staples.

BEACH COMMUNITY BOUNDARIES Many vacation areas, including those along the Florida coast, have restrictive covenants that limit the style, size, and color of new homes. Nellie didn't want a traditional cottage—she wanted a fresh expression of shape and color.

After several inquiries, Nellie heard about Grayton Beach's flexible approach toward architecture. The development's general design guidelines simply suggest that new coastal cottages have pale exterior beach colors and galvanized-metal roofs, and that they be built in a southern vernacular shape. Those regulations made it easy for this cream-colored plantation-style house, with orange tile accents, to fit well into the community.

Corner windows in the dining area and the wraparound veranda beyond open up the space and frame long, diagonal views of the waterway.

The second-floor veranda is where the home owners spend a lot of their time. Here they can dine alfresco and enjoy the sunset in the glow of candlelight. Sturdy metal cable railings seem to disappear against the view of the water below.

the clear Floridian sunsets. And on cool nights when breezes off the Gulf of Mexico carry a chill through the house, its always comforting to huddle around the fire.

A Private Floor

The couple's bedroom, also located on the top floor and down a long hallway away from the living spaces, offers the homeowners some privacy, while children and guests stay one level below.

There's plenty of space on the lower level, including two large bedrooms and a children's playroom, all of which are easily accessible from the front foyer and backyard. To keep the house clean and dry—and so no one has to worry about tracking in sand from the shore—the laundry room is located right off the foyer. Everyone can drop off beach gear for washing and drying before going any farther. It's just the sort of beach house amenity needed after a day spent on the white sands of Grayton Beach.

A Wilderness Perch with Harbor Views

Built in the spirit of National Park Service fire towers, this simple wood and glass retreat provides unparalleled views along the coast of the San Juan Islands.

The panoramic view from this tiny cabin overlooking the water is all that Joe and Peg Erskine require of their getaway. The Erskines, an active family who likes to camp and navigate the rugged terrain of national parks, realized the type of vacation place they sought was one that would allow them to take refuge high above the sea. But they also wanted a site that would make the family feel as though they were on an adventure every time they traveled to the retreat from their Seattle home. In response, architect David Vandervort designed a simple 700-sq.-ft. coastal cabin that rests high on a peak overlooking the San Juan Islands, accessible only by foot through forested terrain.

The cabin's back deck is the perfect viewing platform for the frequent nighttime meteor showers that rain down over San Juan Bay.

Tucked under a sleeping loft at one end of this back-to-basics cabin, the kitchen is designed to be just one step up from a campsite kitchen. A salvaged piece of marble serves as the countertop, and the kitchen has no running water: The Erskines bring their own bottles of water up to the retreat.

The walls of the cabin are exposed cedar sheathing to blend in with the surrounding environment. The rustic interior, along with the indoor picnic table, makes the homeowners feel as though they were eating outdoors. The table can be easily moved out to the deck for alfresco dining.

Standing Securely on the Land

Although the wood and glass cabin looks primitive in its design, it is held to the land by sophisticated technologies that keep the twin-tower structure securely anchored high above the coastline. Since the ground beneath the cabin is mostly rock and shallow soil, the structure is tied to the site by steel rebar (concrete-reinforcing steel bars) that is drilled into the ancient rock ledge. The cabin also sits on concrete piers sunk into the earth.

Anchoring the structure to the ground was only one challenge posed by the site—wind shear was another. To keep the sometimes unrelenting wind from damaging the building, the lower floors of the two tower-like structures are reinforced with a sheathing of rigid insulation sandwiched between panels of plywood to increase stability. With solid, well-anchored towers at either end, the central one-story link between them could be more transparent, featuring window walls that allow a clear view to the water straight through the middle of the cabin.

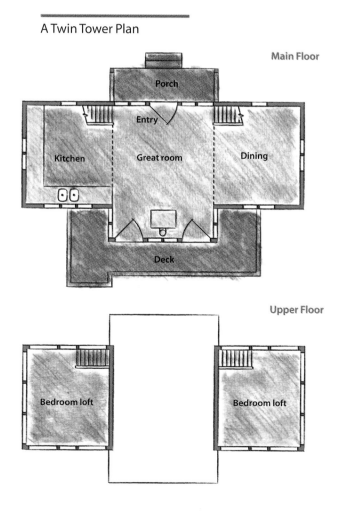

A Twin Tower Plan

Main Floor

Porch

Entry

Kitchen   Great room   Dining

Deck

Upper Floor

Bedroom loft   Bedroom loft

A single woodstove warms up the entire cabin. From this spot, the distant city lights of Victoria can be seen through the window wall of the central living space, while a band of transom windows above helps lift the ceiling toward the sky.

This remote cabin sits atop natural rock outcrop. The homeowners park, then hike up the hill to get to the house along a path hidden among native cedar trees.

Back to Basics

The openness of the plan and the large number of windows in this small space is intentional, creating a sort of indoor camping atmosphere. The two towers with second-floor lofts—one with a bedroom for adults, the other for children—are located at opposite ends of the cabin but are open to one another. This arrangement lets the whole family see and talk with each other. Despite its openness, the getaway feels cozy. The glass box in the middle of the structure is just large enough for a living room with a futon, a no-frills kitchen outfitted with a propane refrigerator and range, and a dining space defined by a weathered picnic table.

The Erskines, who spent years roughing it in sleeping bags on this property, love vacationing in an unspoiled spot on top of the world, where they have few more comforts than camping equipment. From their cabin, the family can catch a glimpse of Victoria on a clear day, hear distant fog horns and night owls, and still be the first to greet the glorious sunrise of each new day.

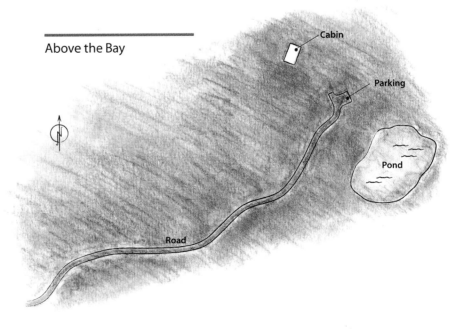

Above the Bay

Cabin

Parking

Pond

Road

N

From top to bottom, the cabin is designed for stability. Galvanized-metal roofs provide a durable, protective top, while exposed concrete piers under the cabin tether the structure to the land.

A PICTURESQUE OUTLOOK The Erskine family camped on the 7-acre piece of land for nearly a decade before building their permanent cabin. During that time, Joe built a multilevel covered viewing platform where they were able to camp while enjoying the distant views of Mount Baker. It was the view that encouraged the family time and time again to make the vigorous 4-hour trek from their home in Seattle. After a drive, a ferry ride, a second drive, and a hike (with a weekend's worth of supplies strapped to their backs), the family would finally reach the platform. Even today, there's still no better place to watch the Fourth of July fireworks displays set off in the towns that surround the island.

Simplicity above the Dunes

The sunsets are priceless, but a simple design and basic materials made this beach house come in within the homeowners' budget.

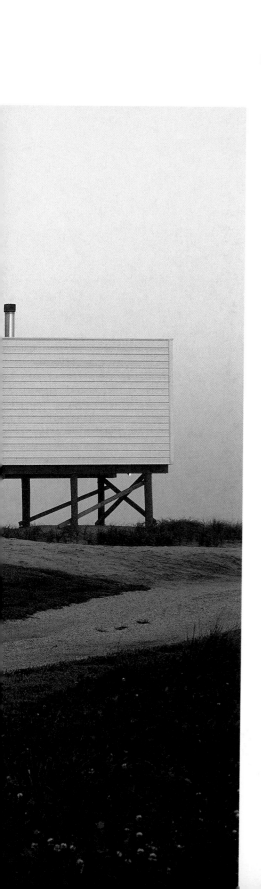

THOUGH IT'S HARD TO BELIEVE, IT IS POSSIBLE TO BUILD AN

inexpensive hideaway on a slice of sand in a popular beach community.

When Ken Kuchin and Bruce Anderson bought one of the last undeveloped

oceanfront parcels in much sought-after East Hampton, they wanted to

build a simple getaway where they could find some privacy, entertain, and

enjoy the gusty breezes coming off the Atlantic Ocean. Local architect

Preston Philips helped the homeowners achieve their dream with a

1,000-sq.-ft. beach house on wood piers that crafts utilitarian materials into

spaces reminiscent of the modernist beach cottages of the 1950s and 1960s.

**The living room's soaring 20-ft.-tall windows let sun pour in
all day and moonlight shine in all night. The windows also
frame the view of the ocean, which is just steps away.**

The walkway's gentle upward slope from the road to the house is designed to create a long, gradual approach to an anticipated panoramic view of the ocean.

A pergola tops part of the deck to create a shaded outdoor room. From the pergola, there is a view of the two shed-style rooflines that delineate the living room space. These whimsical "butterfly wings" are nearly 6 ft. higher than the other rooflines of the house.

Built on Piers

Ken and Bruce wanted the house sited so that it would put them as close as possible to the water while still being protected from the elements. Wood piers lift the house above the dunes so it peeks out over the sandbanks, giving the homeowners uninterrupted views.

It was more than just a pragmatic idea to lift the house up 7 ft. off the sand—and away from potential flooding damage. The homeowners can see the water from beneath the house even as they walk up to it from the road. But when they reach the top of the entrance ramp, they get a breathtaking view of the beach and ocean. The view is so magnificent that they often pause for a few moments to take it in before dropping their luggage indoors.

Carefree Living

Because the homeowners entertain often, they wanted the house to be the kind of place where their friends would never worry about bringing in sand from the beach or hanging wet swimsuits in the wrong place. To make the beach house casual and relaxed, the design uses hardy basic building materials, available from local building supply stores.

The exterior of the house is covered with metal barn siding and the deck railings are made from PVC piping, two materials that stand up well to the salt air. The entrance ramp, walkways, and pavilion are all made of inexpensive exterior-grade plywood that will weather well in the misty, moist beach environment.

Indoors, whitewashing the walls eliminated the inherent reddish pink hue of interior-grade plywood while at the same time brightening the rooms. To add color to the living room, blue vinyl wallpaper covers the ceiling, creating the illusion that the ocean is reflected inside.

The bedroom feels serene thanks to the white-washed plywood walls and sisal carpeting. Cork flooring adds to the casual tone of the interior. Windows placed low on the wall give the homeowners ocean views even when they're lounging in bed.

The main entry leads directly into the kitchen. The homeowners prefer space for socializing, rather than for cooking, so they opted for a small kitchen area without costly overhead cabinets.

The living room, in the middle of the house, has an unusual V-shaped ceiling. Soaring to 20 ft. high on either side, it seems as though the living room projects into the outdoors. The bedroom is located beyond the plaster fireplace.

T E R R A I N

It is a challenge to build on a parcel of property that consists of shifting sand dunes and fragile natural vegetation. The kind of concrete foundations that are standard in new construction today erode over time when subject to saltwater flooding. Beach houses on the dunes, like Ken and Bruce's getaway, are often built on a series of wooden piers driven into the sand and reinforced with concrete and metal bars. The East Hampton house is securely lifted 7 ft. off the ground by such piers and by a wood foundation that is stabilized by wood legs with cross bracing.

Three Distinct Spaces

Since the beach house is designed primarily for short overnight stays, the homeowners need only three indoor spaces to be comfortable. The small kitchen, large living room, and generous-size bedroom flow into one another and make up the floor plan of the one-story house. For added privacy, a large plaster fireplace flanked by short hallways separates the bedroom from the rest of the interior.

There's barely any separation between the interior and the exterior, however. Numerous windows frame the outdoor spectacle of the sea, eliminating the need for art or other decor on the walls. The interior provides basic creature comforts of shelter, while most of the relaxation happens on the expansive deck.

The home's prefinished white aluminum siding shines bright on a high spot that rises above the dunes.

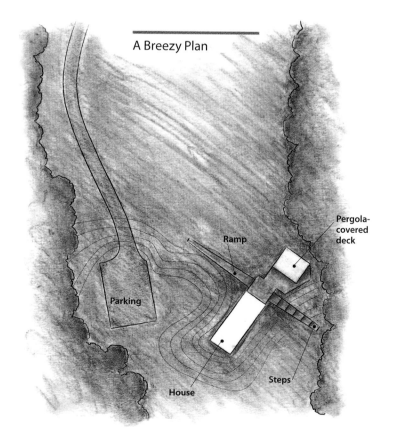

A Breezy Plan

Pergola-covered deck

Ramp

Parking

House

Steps

A Double-Duty Deck

One of the hallmarks of beach house design is outdoor living, and there is no shortage of exterior space for relaxing in this getaway. The long and linear deck doubles the size of the beach house, and it feels like an outdoor room because a pergola caps part of the space.

The house's design—from the deck to the butterfly roof—is a departure from that of the elaborate shingle-style homes nearby. This different approach is intentional because the homeowners' goal was simplicity, and this house gives them all they need for a comfortable stay above the dunes.

A Neighborhood with Ocean Views

A low wooden picket fence and bushes enclose the front yard, helping preserve a bit of privacy and providing a visual clue that the main entryway is located elsewhere.

O

LD MEMORIES CAN FUEL THE DESIRE TO FIND THE PERFECT

getaway. That's what drove one homeowner to build a dream beach cottage

in a historic, close-knit neighborhood in Santa Cruz. Al Crema never had

the chance for beach-time recreation during his busy college days, and as an

adult he longed to vacation in a house on the water where he could gather

friends, family, and neighbors together for frequent gourmet meals.

Al bought what seemed like the ideal beachfront property. The existing

house, however, was in need of major repairs. Before the work could be

completed, an earthquake all but demolished the structure, creating an

This cottage on Santa Cruz Bay is a 2,800 sq.-ft. home, but it doesn't look it. The house was designed to appear smaller than it is, since it occupies such a small lot. The mandatory off-street garage is tucked back on the side of the house, minimizing its visual impact.

A second-floor deck extends the living space in the upstairs family room. It's a place where the family often gathers for stargazing.

opportunity to build anew. But the lot is small, 40 ft. wide and 120 ft. deep, and located in a historic area where most new architecture blends with the old. Architect Tom Thatcher created a new house in keeping with the fabric of the established neighborhood, while keeping in mind the homeowner's contemporary wish list for a large kitchen, room for visiting family and friends, and veranda with a view to the ocean.

The house next door is not as tall as the Cremas' home, so the couple has a view from their bedroom across the neighbor's rooftop.

New Old Beach House

Older houses in the neighborhood typically have wood lap siding, bracketed overhangs, and sloping rooflines, and the Cremas' house is no different. The traditional two-story house has a front porch punctuated by tapered wood columns in the Arts and Crafts style.

But inside, the home reveals itself as a contemporary beach house with an open floor plan and light cherry wood cathedral ceilings. Not only is the interior bright and airy, but it's also designed so the dining room is a step up from the living room, giving each space unobstructed views to the ocean.

Because the house is located on a busy street with a lot of foot traffic, it was designed with a number of semiprivate outdoor spaces, including a second-floor porch and a courtyard off the kitchen. Surrounded by a high fence at the back of the house, the courtyard is a natural extension of the cooking area and the setting for the feasts and gatherings this getaway was designed to host.

This getaway isn't all about the beach. On the back side of the house, a bay window in the kitchen overlooks a well-used, casual dining area on the rear courtyard.

View to the Bay

Main Floor

Main entry

Dining room

Kitchen

Veranda

Living room

Courtyard

Garage

Bedroom

Laundry

PART THREE

In the Mountains

THEIR MOUNTAIN

GETAWAY BRINGS

INDOORS THE BEAUTY

OF MOUNTAIN VIEWS

AND A LANDSCAPE

OF WEATHERED

PASTURELAND. . . .

THE HOME FOLLOWS

THE STEPPED

CONTOURS OF

THE LAND.

A Modern Barn on the Mountainside

The homeowners' love of the mountains and their passion for the region's outdoor activities led them to build a getaway in a golf community in the Colorado Rockies.

A WELL-TENDED MOUNTAINSIDE GOLF RESORT MAY SEEM LIKE AN unusual backdrop for a rustic barn-style getaway. But it doesn't seem so to Doug and Linda Hacker, a couple from Chicago who thought a simple structure would be all they needed during busy weekends filled with skiing, snowboarding, and fishing. To suit their informal vacationing lifestyle, architect Harry Teague designed a holiday home with roughsawn siding, log columns, and a limestone foundation that's meant to look like a Colorado hay barn sitting alongside a newly mowed mountainside meadow.

The living spaces in this getaway are upstairs. A large glass window wall at the top of the steps stamps a contemporary imprint onto the barn-style architecture.

The kitchen windows look out over the seventh tee, down the fairway, and straight to the snow-capped mountains.

Home on the Golf Range

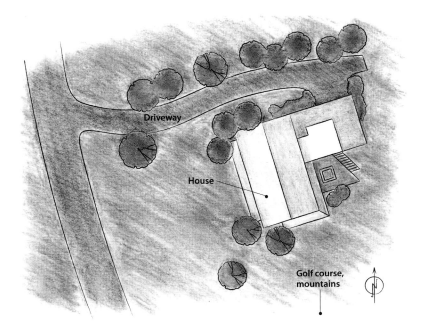

Driveway

House

Golf course, mountains

N

A Design from Times of Yore

There's a reason for the rustic design. The golf community sits on the land of a former ranch where there were hay barns aplenty. A hay barn, also known as a pole barn, is a type of regional roofed structure without walls, meant to keep stored hay dry. The new barn-style house harkens back to those earlier rustic structures. Its peaked roof shape also mirrors 13,000-ft.-high Mount Sopris, which rises up from the valley floor and dominates the landscape.

The same basic materials used to build barns—wood, steel, and stone—give this house its authentic sensibility. Cedar shakes cover the roof, and two lower-level bump-outs look like lean-tos on a farmhouse. Within the framework of the barn-inspired design, large expanses of glass replace sections of wall, modernizing the style while providing a view to the majestic landscape.

The southeast corner of the house has a deck with stairs to a hot tub, which gets full morning sun and has direct access from the lower-level master bedroom behind it.

Selecting materials for this getaway was a hands-on experience for the homeowners. The posts used to create the pole-barn structure were made from dead but still standing lodgepole pines that they harvested from a nearby national forest. They have fond memories of their young son scrambling around in a foot of snow helping drag the trees to the road for pick up. One of the tree trunks is now a structural post in his bedroom.

Most of the west side of the house is a wall of glass so the homeowners can watch the sunsets from the living room or from the recessed balcony. Below the balcony, one of the bedroom bump-outs has a galvanized metal roof, much like that of a barn.

A MODERN BARN ON THE MOUNTAINSIDE

The interior layout of the house also has a barnlike feel. Traditional barn floor plans have an open upper level, much like a loft, filled with hay and streaming sun, and a main floor that's stanchioned off with feeding bins and animal stalls, kept calm with muted light. To capture coveted views for the places where they'll be most enjoyed, the living space is on the top floor and the bedrooms are located on the lower level. By placing all the rooms that need privacy on the lower level, the main floor retains an open, light-filled floor plan. To complement the character of the house, a strong rural decorating theme is used throughout the house.

A Ranch Hand's Refuge

Although the house is new, the interior looks like an old barn converted to living space. Roughsawn wood walls throughout the house are held up by oversize, exposed structural timbers. The brick flooring in the kitchen feels like it might have been found in a ranch hand's retreat. And outside the multipurpose room on the lower level, a pair of large, sliding barn doors closes off the space when television or social activities get too loud.

Whether the Hackers are lounging inside or out, the design of their getaway gives them a solid connection to the region's rich rural history and the glorious recreational setting.

The stairwell is divided from the foyer by a set of vertical slats, designed to look like the walls of a barn's corncrib, that let in light while still separating the spaces.

Bottom Floor Privacy

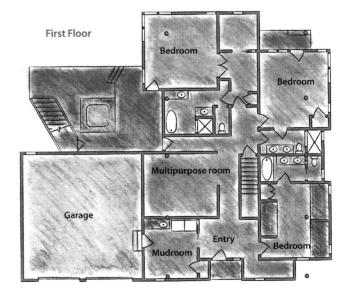

First Floor

Bedroom

Bedroom

Multipurpose room

Garage

Mudroom

Entry

Bedroom

The living spaces on the top level have uninterrupted views of the mountainside scenery. Since the roof is held up by a pole-barn style structure, there is no need for load-bearing interior walls.

Wild sage inspired the color of the painted kitchen cabinets. The teal color complements the earthen tones of the brick floor.

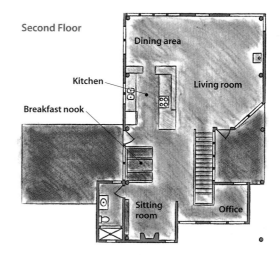

Second Floor

Dining area

Kitchen

Living room

Breakfast nook

Sitting room

Office

A Cabin with a Story

A long, winding driveway wraps around the meadow in front of the cabin. The garage is angled so it is not the first thing the homeowners see as they approach the residence.

W

ILLIE DRAKE HAS A PASSION FOR SALVAGED WOOD, WHICH

he's been seeking out and selling for more than 30 years. So when he and his

wife decided to build their own mountain getaway and to spend more time

fly-fishing, it was a natural decision to recycle wood that Willie had gathered

from dismantled buildings all over the country.

With its green shingled roof and dark brown cypress siding, the house,

designed by architect John Dalgleish, has a fitting rural design for a West

Virginia retreat, where fly-fishing in Fish Hatchery Run and Shaver's Fork

River is the region's most popular activity.

**A kiva-style stone fireplace constructed of local
river rock and dry-laid mountain stones warms the
covered porch in the cooler seasons.**

A Pair of Porches

Blending seamlessly into the woods that surround it, the cabin was designed to take advantage of the beauty of the site. Two porches—one on the front and one on the back of the house—provide ample outdoor living space for the Drakes' enjoyment of the woodland setting.

A four-season sun porch overlooking the side yard and pond is located off the living room. Adjacent to this porch is a more casual covered porch on the side of the house. Its built-in benches let homeowners and guests comfortably gather around the hearth when there's a chill in the air. From this redwood and cypress porch, there are long views across the meadow to the side and the front of the house, where the Drakes can bask in the morning sun and greet guests as they come and go.

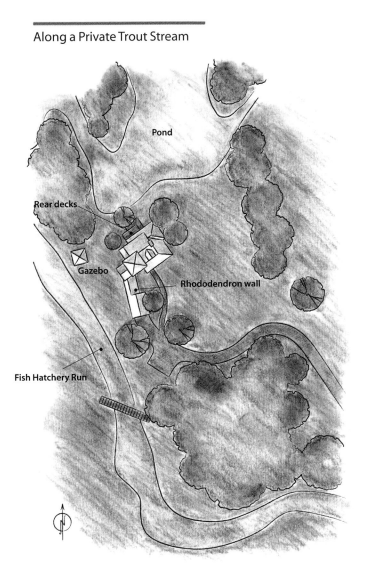

Along a Private Trout Stream

Pond

Rear decks

Gazebo

Rhododendron wall

Fish Hatchery Run

An old metal star from the outside wall of a textile mill is displayed above the window of the second-floor sitting room. These types of stars were used in 19th-century brick buildings to secure the ends of long rods that helped stabilize the structure.

The oversize double-hung windows in the four-season sun porch ensure unobstructed views of the pond.

The garage, connected to the house by a small shop, looks like a diminutive barn.

The stairway, including the newel post, is made of heart pine that came from a historic train station in Charlottesville, Virginia.

A Place with Extra Space

First Floor

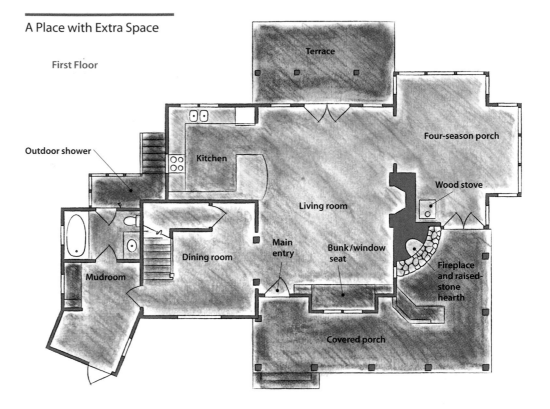

Terrace

Four-season porch

Outdoor shower

Kitchen

Wood stove

Living room

Main entry

Bunk/window seat

Dining room

Fireplace and raised-stone hearth

Mudroom

Covered porch

The getaway has only two bedrooms, but there's no lack of space for guests. Oversize window seats throughout the house double as beds, including built-ins on the third floor of the tower, where guests can wake up to a 360-degree view of the property.

Second Floor

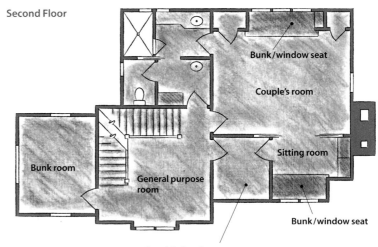

Bunk/window seat

Couple's room

Sitting room

Bunk room

General purpose room

Bunk/window seat

Couple's dressing room

A pass-through between the wood-sided kitchen and the dining room makes the kitchen feel larger than it is. The lighter tone wood used for the ceiling brings an abundance of reflected sunlight deep into the space.

Creating an Easy Flow

Multiple entryways on different sides of the house make it possible to glide effortlessly between indoors and outdoors. The main entrance, tucked under the covered porch on the south side of the property, opens directly into a casual living room. The path flows easily from the front door through the living space, out the French doors, and onto the terrace overlooking the backyard pond.

The kitchen and dining room are close to the garage, making it easy to unload groceries, luggage, and supplies. Both rooms open directly into the living room so that everyone can enjoy one another's company, whether they're cooking, snacking, or relaxing.

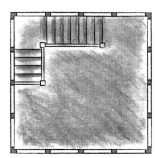

Towering Views through the Trees

The most private part of the house is the tower, which rises into the treetops. Located in the center of the house, it's where the Drakes get their best views of the property. The dining room forms the base of the tower, and an L-shaped staircase works its way up to the second floor. The second floor of the tower space serves as a general-purpose room and central hallway from which the bedrooms, including the couple's suite, spin off.

The third floor of the tower was originally going to be the couple's retreat, but they decided to make it a common area (and auxiliary sleeping space) so that everyone can enjoy the 360-degree views of the surrounding landscape. All day, sunlight pours into the room through windows on all four sides. The combination of scenery and natural light makes the top of the tower a magical place, lifting the Drakes and their guests above the treetops and giving them private views of their own cold-water trout stream.

The homeowners wanted to preserve a wall of rhododendron plants that line the banks of the stream. The tower evolved as a way to have views of the stream without damaging the landscape.

THE SECRET LIFE OF WOOD If these walls could talk, the Drakes' cabin would have quite a few stories to tell. Willie wanted to showcase his collection of salvaged wood, and this cabin seemed like the natural place for it. So he embedded history into the walls and floors through his choice of woods. The flooring in the house is distressed southern heart pine rescued from a cold-storage building in Rhode Island. Kitchen cabinets and living room wall paneling were milled from American chestnut salvaged from West Virginia barns. And the ceilings throughout are supported by purlins and beams from Boston-area textile mills.

The property has two log footbridges, including one that crosses Fish Hatchery Run and another that reaches over a small creek. The quiet of the still pond in front of the cabin contrasts with the turbulence of "the run."

A House in the Sun

Deep overhangs help keep the high summer sun out of this New Mexico getaway. The west-facing living/dining area is sheltered by a veranda but open to a flagstone patio.

as their refuge from their New York City apartment, John and Polly Barton's

family grew and so did their love of the desert. They began to transform a

solar-powered seasonal retreat into a year-round house by building a round

annex connected to the original house by an outdoor terrace. The Bartons

call this desert hideaway "Casa Mirasol," which means House of the

Beautiful Sun.

From the half-mile-long driveway that gently rises and falls with the

landscape, the house—despite its distinct shape and 3,000 sq. ft. of living

space—is barely discernable in the distance. Because both parts of the

retreat were built in the adobe tradition, the color and texture of this low-

slung house blend seamlessly into the landscape.

From a distance, the house looks like just another mesa.
Seclusion is important to the homeowners, who intentionally
hid the house among the juniper and piñon trees.

The curve of the annex's wall creates a private patio, with a corrugated-steel roof, outside one of the bedrooms.

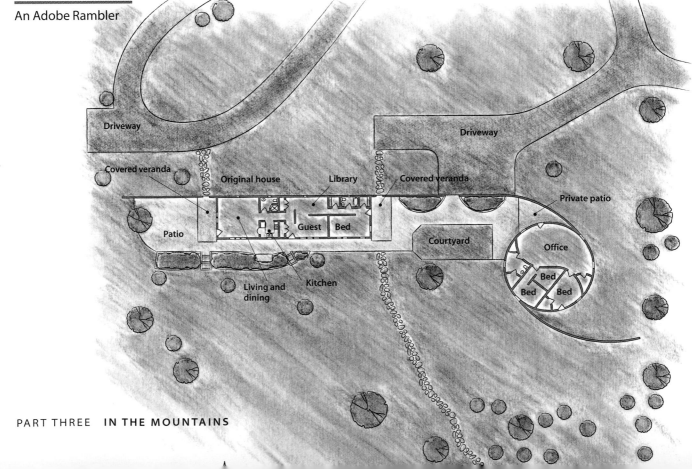

An Adobe Rambler

Driveway

Driveway

Covered veranda

Original house

Library

Covered veranda

Private patio

Patio

Guest

Bed

Courtyard

Office

Living and dining

Kitchen

Bed

Bed

Bed

A Pinwheel in the Sand

The house was sited toward the middle of the couple's long, narrow property to maximize privacy on all sides, but there was plenty of room to add on to accommodate their needs. The original house, a simple 1,600-sq. ft. rectangle, 20 ft. wide by 80 ft. long, was built out of traditional adobe materials. The annex was built with the same materials and in the same adobe tradition. But the homeowners wanted the shape of the new wing to be a departure from the original, and decided to build a circular annex with unique winglike walls that radiate out, like sides of a pinwheel, from a cylinder.

The shape of the annex was chosen to benefit the property in a number of ways. The circular form balances the long, narrow main part of the house. Designing the annex as a separate structure enclosed by two curved walls provided opportunities to create sheltered outdoor patios and verandas. And the tapered ends of the walls help blend the new structure into the landscape while giving it a sense of energy and movement.

IN FOCUS

Adobe, which is made of clay and straw, is porous. The walls of the annex sit on fieldstone bases to prevent moisture from wicking up from the ground and into the adobe.

A gently curved wall between the circular annex and the main house connects the two buildings. There is no indoor connection.

A long hallway with built-in shelving divides the main wing. Cool flagstone flooring is used throughout the house to connect the interior rooms with the exterior spaces.

A freestanding arched adobe wall creates a hallway between the kitchen and library/guest room.

Open-Air Rooms

As there are so many spectacular views surrounding the property—Sangre de Cristo Mountains to the southeast, Jemez Mountains to the west, Black Mesa due south, and a view of Nevada beyond the mesa—the outdoor rooms around the house increase the Bartons' enjoyment of their home. An open-air room connects the main house to the round annex, covered verandas are placed at each end of the main house, and there are two more tucked into the curves of the annex's tapered walls. In addition, there are a number of stone courtyards around the house.

The covered verandas that flank the main house also shield the structure from the low, hot summer sun. The broad overhangs of the porches and windows recessed deep into the thick adobe walls block the sun from baking the interior. The south side of the house has large banks of windows that capture the views of two distinct mountain ranges and the Black Mesa in between. During the winter, the low southern sun comes through the large windows and warms the concrete flooring, which is original to the main house.

An Atypical Annex

The interior of the main house is traditional, with a kitchen, living and dining areas, a couple's bedroom, a library, and a guest bedroom. Across the connecting courtyard and terrace, the round annex creates unique interior spaces. John's office occupies half the space, and

The curving interior of John's office in the annex has heated concrete floors and a woodstove to ensure warmth during winter months. Part of the annex's fieldstone base is left exposed behind the woodstove.

An interior window connects the kitchen and the dining room. The window wall is not typical of adobe houses, but was added in this home to bring the mountain view into the small kitchen.

A MODIFIED PUEBLO The homeowners cherish the culture and landscape that inspired the choice of location for their getaway. The main house was built using traditional adobe techniques and was influenced by the rectilinear style of Pueblo houses. The annex's soft, curvilinear shape was inspired by the Spanish Mission–style churches of the region.

Although authentic Pueblo-style houses in the Southwest are structured as a series of rooms built around a central courtyard, the Bartons' main house is a simple rectangle with large windows along the south side to soak up heat in the winter. When the Bartons first built their house, the location was off the grid, so they could not use traditional electricity. Instead, they relied on photovoltaic solar panels for power and took advantage of passive solar gain for energy efficiency. They even collected and stored rainwater in an underground cistern. Today, the house connects to a regional source of electricity. This powers their new well and allows them to live there year-round.

three bedrooms take up the rest. An S-shaped curving wall divides the two halves and makes the aerial view of the structure look like a yin-yang symbol. It was designed that way for its unique visual impact, but it's an aesthetic gesture that continues the feeling of movement indoors.

There's a sense of serenity threading throughout the hideaway that mixes with the hum of activity. John runs his architectural practice from his half of the circular annex, while in a detached studio near the house Polly designs silk kimonos with a southwestern flair, a result of the influence desert life has on her. Though it took some time for Polly, a native New Yorker, to feel comfortable living beneath the velvet dark, star-filled skies of New Mexico, the wide-open spaces surrounding this full-time oasis serve as a constant inspiration to the once-urban couple.

There are few openings on the north side of the house. Where they occur, they are small, with stone lintels that add character to the adobe structure.

Building a Family Legacy

The couple who built this hideaway raised their four daughters in an urban environment. They chose a mountain setting for their getaway because of the outdoor recreational opportunities and the limitless views.

C RAIG AND DEBORAH BARBER'S FIRST DUDE RANCH VACATION MORE THAN three decades ago was the start of what became an annual family pilgrimage from their home in a busy Midwestern city to the rugged Big-Sky landscape of Montana. After one of their four daughters moved west, the couple followed, building a Craftsman-inspired timber-frame retirement getaway with views of Montana's Bridger Mountains. When they aren't on the go cross-country skiing, mountain biking, or hiking, the Barbers share with their family a home that brings indoors the beauty of mountain views and a landscape of weathered pastureland.

Most important to the Barbers was being able to live comfortably in all the rooms of their new getaway. Architect Katherine Hillbrand achieved this by designing a house that follows the stepped contours of the land.

The lower level of the house has a separate mudroom entrance where family and guests stow skis and other recreational equipment. The upper balcony extends from the couple's bedroom.

125

Mapping Out the House

Each level of the house has an outdoor room connecting the interior to the landscape. The stone terrace off the dining room is covered by a metal arbor.

The architect stood with the homeowners on the roof of the local timber framer's pick-up truck to find the best views, and everyone agreed that the house should be built into the western slope of an open, sun-baked meadow. As a result, in summer the house is surrounded by blooming wildflowers, and in winter it's nestled between constantly shifting snowdrifts. In every season, the couple has views of approaching weather conditions along with a bird's-eye view of the mountain range to the north.

By building the house into the grassy slope of the hill, the architecture enhances a unique landscape. The house is an unusually long and narrow rectangle—80 ft. long by 22 ft. wide. The irregular shape of the house ensures that most rooms have windows on two sides, offering views in at least two directions and cross ventilation from the winds that race across the valley.

A Stepped Floor Plan

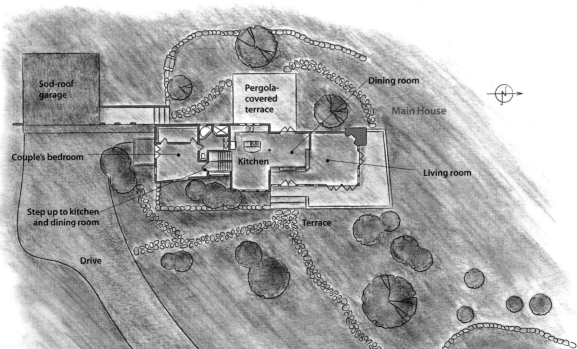

Sod-roof garage

Pergola-covered terrace

Dining room

Main House

Couple's bedroom

Kitchen

Living room

Step up to kitchen and dining room

Terrace

Drive

N

A hallway through the middle of the house connects the main level with the upstairs and downstairs. A flight of stairs goes up to the couple's bedroom suite and office, and another flight of stairs goes down to the guest room and mudroom.

A Six-Level Sanctum

The front entry is recessed into the house to provide protection from the elements. Four identical wood doors make it look like this entrance is the way into a barn.

From a distance, the house seems to emerge from the hillside. The rooms of the 3,200-sq.-ft. home are built on six different levels. Inside, the plan is open, but the spaces jig and jag, with slight elevations up and down from one room to the next. Half a flight down from the kitchen is a guest room, laundry, mudroom, and trellis-covered walkway to the garage. Half a flight up is the couple's bedroom, where morning light streams in through a roof dormer.

The kitchen is in the center of the house, on the main level, elevated for unobstructed views. From there, the cook can see outdoors in three directions—a direct view out to the ranch land from the sink, views through the house to the north-facing terrace, and a view toward the front so the homeowners can see guests coming and going.

Outdoor living spaces placed right outside most rooms ensure that the Barbers don't feel confined indoors. For example, a stone terrace wraps around one corner of the house and is accessible from the living room. A pergola-covered terrace on the west side of the house protects the dining window from the low, hot western sun. It's also a perfect spot for an alfresco dinner.

A poured-concrete sod-roof garage is built into the hillside as a way of reducing the scale of the large structure. The earth surrounding the garage tempers the swings in temperature, an added benefit of building into the hillside.

S N A P S H O T

In ranch-land tradition, a friend of the Barbers gave the family a branded insignia for their hideaway, which is found on the mailbox and on the garage's entrance.

A crooked tree that was harvested from the Barbers' property is used as a structural beam above their bed, paying homage to the wood used in the house's construction. The pole beam stabilizes the wall dividing the bedroom and the closet.

The bird's nest, located at the top of the house, serves as a library, office, and guest sleeping space. The nest is open to the kitchen below, letting the light from the arched window filter down to the lower levels of the house.

Crafted with Care

On their first trip to Montana, the couple fell in love with the rustic Western tradition of using simple, durable materials such as heavy timber-frame beams and local stone. The Barbers took the opportunity to build a house with this handcrafted look, incorporating these elements in a way that complemented the Craftsman furniture they planned to furnish their new home with. Building a sturdy house into the contours of the landscape was all part of an effort to create a getaway that will become a long-lasting legacy, treasured by future generations who visit this majestic landscape.

The couple's room includes a view of the bunk house, convenient when the owners are awaiting late-arriving visitors.

The entry has a place to sit and take off boots. The armoire cabinet is part of the beautiful collection of Craftsman furniture in the house.

A Bit of Italy

During spring, the owners tend the ornamental beds in the formal parterre garden off the guest wing. The hinged wooden shutters were inspired by similar shutters found on Italian villas. They are used to block out the hot summer sun and keep the interior of the house cool.

WHEN A COUPLE FROM WASHINGTON, D.C., DECIDED TO BUILD A

getaway in the country, they returned to the land of their youth: the West

Virginia panhandle. There, they transformed a 20-acre cornfield into a

botanical treasure that reflects their love of northern Italy and their affec-

tion for rural architecture. The character of the retreat, designed by archi-

tects Beth Reador and Chuck Swartz along with landscape architect Brian

Stevenson, is that of a rural Italian compound with a touch of West

Virginia vernacular. Corrugated-metal roofs like those found locally sit

atop smooth stucco walls, a common feature of Italian villas. Doors with

shutters of cedar slats look convincingly Tuscan. And the European

touches complement the classic American red painted garage and its

southern-style dog trot.

The homeowners were drawn to this site because of the views. They built a house with many windows and a screened room looking out over the gently rolling terrain.

New grass and trees supplant the stalks of corn that once grew in this field. The long and winding driveway leads up to the hilltop hideaway.

In the Italian Countryside

The previous agricultural use of the land left the property without very many distinctive features, so the landscape design introduced them, in particular a long, narrow driveway that winds through a corridor of recently planted, evenly spaced trees. The driveway leads to a bold red gatehouse that conceals a courtyard and the main house beyond. The buildings are closely placed around the courtyard, creating a peaceful enclave that conveys a clear sense of arrival. A bubbling fountain and lily pond greet guests as they park.

The gatehouse is designed to look like a barn and functions like one, too. Cars are stored in two bays on one side of the opening and a tractor is parked in a bay on the opposite side. Tucked into one corner of the gatehouse is a potting room and covered porch where the homeowners store gardening tools.

Just across the courtyard is the main house, which looks as though it were lifted from an Italian farm. The house is made up of three connecting buildings, each having about the same square footage but a distinctly different feel.

Focus on **Outdoor** Views

The Old-World feeling continues in the entryway, where there are views through a set of windows in the foyer and a wall of windows in the living room looking out over the river valley to the mountains. The great room, a

The house is visible after you pass through a barnlike gatehouse. Sliding barn doors close for privacy and security, creating a stillness that reminds homeowners and guests that they are leaving everyday life behind.

The owners love the countryside because it gives them ample opportunities to garden. This charming potting shed and porch is part of the gatehouse.

A Gateway to the Gardens

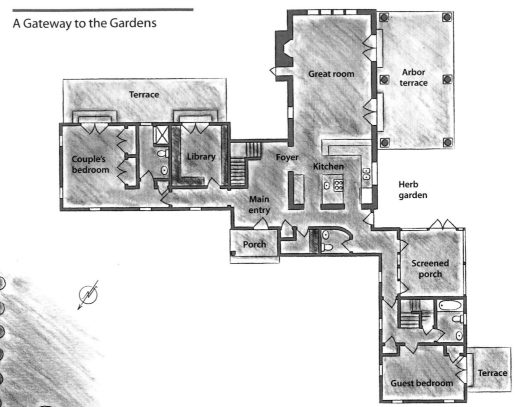

Great room

Arbor terrace

Terrace

Couple's bedroom

Library

Foyer

Kitchen

Herb garden

Main entry

Porch

Screened porch

Guest bedroom

Terrace

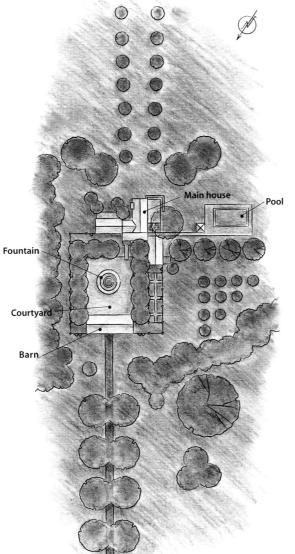

Main house

Pool

Fountain

Courtyard

Barn

In Focus

The living-area pavilion is constructed with split-face concrete block, with rusticated interior walls. The cores of the block are filled with insulation, a way to improve temperature control.

The grandness of the great room is heightened by the large windows that overlook the Potomac River Valley and the foothills of the Blue Ridge Mountains.

combination living room, dining room, and kitchen, is tucked under high ceilings in a building constructed with rough-faced burnished concrete block that has the look of cut stone.

No matter where the homeowners are standing in this house, they can see the gardens. On the right side of the house, the orchard is in full view. The couple's bedroom suite has a terrace with mountain views, the living and dining rooms have an arbor-covered terrace facing west, and the guest bedroom has its own small terrace that looks out over the formal garden. The screened porch overlooks an herb garden and swimming pool.

Just outside the living room's 10-ft.-wide by 10-ft.-high picture window is an allée, a passageway between two rows of evenly spaced cypress trees. Below the living room is the entrance to the exercise room and wine cellar.

An arbor-covered terrace off the great room looks out to the pool and surrounding fields. The natural color and texture of the slate floor connect the outdoor space to the landscape.

Pavilions with Purpose

Each of the three parts of the house has a sense of individual identity, reinforced by a slightly different scale. Yet the buildings are connected to one another. The main entry and foyer connect the living and dining wing to the owner's suite, and a screened porch connects this main living space to the guest quarters. Thus, the great room/pavilion, located between the couple's suite and the guest quarters, maximizes privacy for the owners and their guests. Inside the three buildings, the materials and decor work together, unifying all with the colors and textures of Europe.

The once-barren cornfield is now landscaped using ideas the couple first saw abroad and objects they brought home from their travels. It's easy to see why they feel as if they were vacationing a continent away each time they visit the house. After drying off from a late-afternoon dip in the pool, they're likely to be back in the garden, picking fresh herbs to garnish a great Italian risotto.

GARDEN HOUSE ESSENTIALS The homeowners feel most at home when they are tending their property, so it was fitting to integrate elements of a garden house into this getaway. A garden house is a structure that is connected to the landscape with numerous openings to the outdoors that allow the homeowners to experience the land during different times of the day, from sunrise to sunset. This home has plentiful links to the outdoors—through screened porches, porticos, and terraces that lead to the gardens—making it easy for homeowners and guests to wander out of the house whenever the breeze beckons.

Easy access to the outdoors was first valued in mild climates, but today windows and French doors with good insulation make it possible for those in colder climates to enjoy visual access to nature even when it's too cold to venture outside.

During the summer, the pergola helps filter out the late afternoon sun while homeowners and guests dine alfresco.

A Submerged Ski House in the Snow

The living room of this snow-capped ski house is a bright, sunny space that captures the southern sun. The floors throughout the house are made of karri, a dark, rich Australian wood that is hard enough to withstand the heavy traffic of ski boots.

T HE IDEA OF A SKI-HOUSE GETAWAY OFTEN BRINGS WITH IT

visions of cozy evenings spent around the fireplace while snow falls softly

all around. One family took the dream a step further when they decided to

build a house where annual snowfall sometimes exceeds 12 ft. Located three

hours from their house in San Francisco and 7,000 ft. above sea level in the

Sierra Nevada mountains, this getaway is in a remote area called Sugar

Bowl, part of a resort founded in the late 1930s by Walt Disney, who wanted

the village to replicate the charm of the European Alps.

During heavy snows, it is hard to tell that this is a three-story house. The remote mountainside site has limited access during the winter, and is near land that the U.S. Forest Service has designated as permanently undeveloped territory.

141

Four metal "trees" hold up the steep-pitched roof above the living room, atrium, and kitchen. The limbs of the trees spread out to handle the heavy snow load that gathers on the roof rafters.

Standing Tall

Bottom Floor

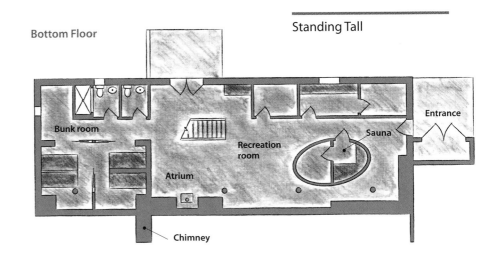

Bunk room

Atrium

Recreation room

Sauna

Entrance

Chimney

The house has several fire-places, including one in the couple's bedroom. An interior window from the stairwell lets light stream into the couple's room.

The retreat is small, private, and so secluded that the only way to get there is to strap on a backpack and ride up the mountain on a snow cat, cable gondola, or snowmobile. The hardy hideaway is not only durable enough to withstand the wet and heavy snowfall, it is also tough enough to endure heavy use from kids, dogs, and wet ski equipment that is constantly being carried in and out of the house's three levels of living space. Since the house is often buried in snow, there are three entrances—one on the top level for when snow is deepest, an entrance in the middle that's used during most of the ski season, and an entry at the lower level used whenever it's accessible.

Catching the Winter Sun

To get the best winter sun and unobstructed views of the mountainside, architect Mark Horton put the main living spaces—living room, dining room, kitchen, and reading nook—on the top floor of the house. The rooms open up to one another under a steeply sloping ceiling, and tall windows direct the eyes upward to the outdoor views. The homeowners and their guests spend most of their time here, where they have the highest vantage point.

Middle Floor

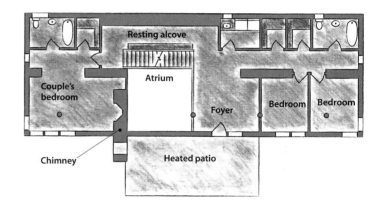

Top Floor

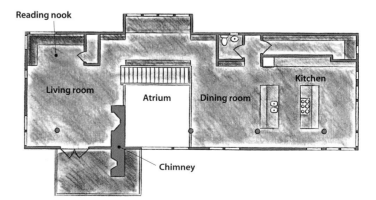

A wall of windows in the third-floor reading alcove offers privacy from nearby cabins. A single transparent window set among the others maintains a connection to the outdoors.

IN FOCUS

In the event of an earthquake, avalanche, or mudslide, the massive concrete chimney would play an important role in maintaining the structural integrity of this snow-engulfed ski house. It's designed to buttress the taller side of the house against forces that could jeopardize a mountainside home.

The couple's suite and a pair of guest rooms occupy the middle level. A small resting alcove overlooking the atrium separates the couple's room from the guest quarters. A foyer off the resting alcove opens up to a patio—the main deep-snow entryway—with an outdoor fireplace, which is often used by those taking a break from the slopes.

A bunk room, a multipurpose recreation room, and another entryway—used when there's little snow—are located on the bottom level. A zinc-sheathed sauna stands in the middle of the large recreation room. The three-story-high atrium window on the south side of the house visually connects all three floors and filters light down into the lower levels when snow covers the windows.

Contemporary Ski Chalet

The house gets much of its contemporary personality from the colorful, textured stained wood, concrete, and steel used both indoors and out. Inside, wood paneling and floors warm up and complement the sculptural steel and jarrah wood (an exotic species of

The bunk room on the lower level doesn't have any windows, but a pair of doors opens to let light into the bedroom from the atrium above. The sauna is beyond the staircase on the right.

hardwood from Australia), which wraps around the smooth-faced concrete fireplace.

Outside, the upper third of the house is sided in Alaskan yellow cedar, which was milled with ribs, or fins, to suggest the log siding of a cabin. A matte black zinc roof was chosen because it easily sheds snow. In harsh weather, it outlasts other materials.

The design of this mountainside getaway protects the homeowners, while at the same time letting them feel as if they lived inside the snowy landscape. They've got confidence in their sturdy house. When they close it up at the end of each visit, they never worry about what natural events might affect their snowcapped getaway once they leave the mountainside.

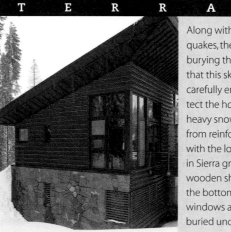

TERRAIN

Along with the risk of earthquakes, the threat of snow burying the house meant that this ski house had to be carefully engineered. To protect the house from tall and heavy snow drifts, it is built from reinforced concrete, with the lower levels wrapped in Sierra granite. A stationary wooden shutter system on the bottom level buffers windows and doors often buried under snow.

PART FOUR

By the Lake

THIS WAS THE

KIND OF PLACE

THEY HAD IN MIND

FOR THEIR GETAWAY—

THE SHORES OF A

COOL STREAM-FED

LAKE IN THE

FOOTHILLS OF

THE MOUNTAINS.

Celebrating the Forces of Nature

The gently sloping property has 300 ft. of shoreline. The irregular shape of the cabin takes advantage of the water views—the longest side and tallest end of the building face the lake.

F

IVE DAYS AFTER DAVID AND SALLY GREGORY KOHLSTEDT BOUGHT

a magnificent, pine-studded lot on a pristine lake, a fierce storm blew

through and leveled almost every tree on the site, leaving behind a tangle of

fallen tree trunks. The Kohlstedts contemplated whether they'd still build

their getaway, because the once-wooded site near the U.S.-Canadian border

had been so transformed. But when architect Dale Mulfinger visited shortly

after the blow-down, he was touched by the visual cacophony and was

inspired to design a cabin in response to what he saw.

The couple, both geology professors in Minnesota, had chosen the

property for its topographical drama and view of the lake. Now, the two

astute observers of the earth's majestic beauty are witness to another

The irregular-shaped cabin
tapers to a 13-ft.- wide point at
the dining room/kitchen end of
the building, yet two walls of
glass doors and windows help
ease any feeling of constriction.
A small patio outside the dining
room is perched on an overlook,
an ideal spot for sunset views.

The walls of the guest loft are examples of the many trapezoidal shapes found in this cabin. The two interior windows on the front wall give visitors privacy while letting light stream in from the rooms below.

A Tapered Plan

Kitchen

Couple's bedroom

Dining area

Stairway

Living area

Porch

Main Level

natural wonder: the cycle of recovery as the forest regenerates. The cabin itself is a fusion of contrasting shapes, creating a memorial to the tempest that will endure even when traces of the storm's wrath can no longer be seen in the surrounding land.

The Legacy of Chaos

The Kohlstedts' original idea had been to build a simple one-bedroom cabin with a loft. From the driveway, the getaway looks like a traditional cabin with a screened porch. But up close, it's evident that the cabin is no simple rectangle but a whimsical trapezoid—a visual statement meant to honor the storm's impact on the site.

Colors and materials used on the exterior of the cabin also give a nod to nature. The forest-green siding reflects new growth found in the midst of now-gray wood downed in the wake of the storm. The window trim and braces under the roof overhangs on one side of the cabin are red, inspired by the birch foundlings in the forest. And one corner of the front porch is held up by

Large windows grouped together in the middle of the living room wall were designed to capture long views of the lake like framed pictures hanging on the wall.

a 6-ft. section of a tree trunk from the site, recalling the downed forest left behind.

Unconventional Interior

The main entrance into the cabin is through the screened porch, which has views of both the lake and the woods. The porch is a popular sitting area, but it also functions as a place to stow coolers and fishing equipment. The porch opens to the living room, which has a tall ceiling that rises to two-story height. Along one wall of the living room a staircase goes up to a small loft at the narrow end of the trapezoid.

The floor plan creates a mix of open and intimate spaces in the 1,300-sq.-ft. cabin. The unusual placement of the rooms is intentional. The dining room feels intimate since it's tucked under the loft at the tapered back end of the cabin. The couple's bedroom is placed in the front of the cabin in the widest part of the floor plan so it's convenient for dropping off suitcases before entering the rest of the space. The bedroom is also placed at the front so it doesn't interrupt the view from the living and dining room. Even with the cabin's unusual angles and surprising architectural elements, the space is inviting and warm.

Materials with a Message

The natural wood finish of the knotty pine walls and birch plywood ceiling create a joyful feeling inside. The wood connects the interior to the surrounding landscape while offering protection and refuge for those seeking rest and relaxation. Even the slate flooring looks like the native ledge rock right outside the windows.

For two scientists passionate about evolution, the view through the floor-to-ceiling windows toward new growth amid the jumble of felled tree limbs is a gratifying sight. That these windows are arranged in an unconventional manner pays tribute to the unpredictable forces that created the scene beyond.

A New Porch Cabin

This lakeside porch cabin looks like an antique, but it's newly built. The property's three buildings—this porch cabin, a garage, and a renovated boathouse—are all sided with white clapboard and detailed with traditional dark green trim to make them look as though they'd been there for generations.

Meg Sirianni's life. Nearly every summer weekend from the time she was five

years old, Meg's parents would pack the kids into the station wagon for a

four-hour drive to the family's log-sided getaway cabin in western Wisconsin.

With three children of her own and sweet memories of childhood summers

still fresh in her mind, she asked architect Dale Mulfinger to design a cottage

reminiscent of the cabin where she spent such happy times with her family.

Meg's own oasis is on a wooded lot just across the lake from her

parents' storybook cabin. Relying in part on Dale's many years studying

traditional cabin architecture, together they designed a vacation home that

fulfills Meg's dreams.

Life at the lake tends to revolve around the beach or the dock, where it's common to find homeowners and guests fishing or just watching the sunset. This wraparound porch connects the house to the water, creating a social place that feels at once indoors and out.

The living room is in the middle of the cabin surrounded by smaller rooms. Since there are no windows to bring in direct light, several interior windows are positioned to filter light from adjacent spaces. Hundred-year-old fir beams and the fieldstone chimney fill the new cabin with a sense of history.

Overlooking the Lake

Lake

Cabin

Dock

Garage rec room

Guest cabin

Living on the Porch

The 2,000-sq.-ft. cabin, though modest by many second-home standards, has plenty of room for guests. To accommodate get-togethers, the screened porch wraps around three sides of the cabin and is the largest space in the house.

The design of the porch was inspired by cabins of the early 1900s. Old-fashioned porch cabins let weekenders visiting from the city sit outside and enjoy the country-fresh air, even if it rained all weekend long. At Meg's cabin, the crackling fire may draw guests into the living room during the coolest weather, but the porch is where visitors spend most of their time, whether it's napping or watching from afar while the kids play near the lake.

Built-in Privacy

The cabin's design accommodates family and friends, yet the Siriannis and their guests can always find an intimate space for some quiet time and solitude. The living room, nestled in the center of the cabin, is large but serves as a cozy gathering spot because it's wrapped

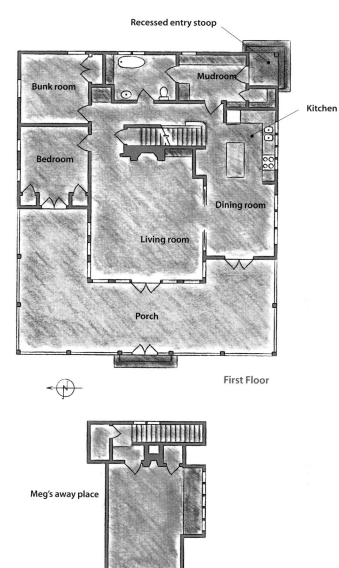

An Updated Porch Plan

Recessed entry stoop

Bunk room · Mudroom · Kitchen · Bedroom · Dining room · Living room · Porch

First Floor

N

Meg's away place

Second Floor

CARRYING ON TRADITION Architect Dale Mulfinger worked with Meg to create a porch cabin that would look like the ones city dwellers of the 1900s built "up north"—along the shores of the Great Lakes and near the many smaller waterways that dot the U.S.'s northern perimeter in the Midwest. They built cabins with large screened porches that became the primary living—and sleeping—areas. Other rooms in these antique cabins were usually small living and sleeping spaces and a compact kitchen and dining room.

Just below the overhead kitchen cabinets there's a sliding window opening into the pantry. A counter on both sides of the window makes it easy to pass groceries between the two rooms. To the left of the refrigerator, an open staircase makes a perfect place to sit and talk.

in wood—flooring, walls, and ceiling—and illuminated with subdued lighting. Other smaller rooms, such as the dining area, kitchen, bunk room, and back hallway, surround the living space, adding to its protected feeling.

Meg's original plan was to have her bedroom near the porch, but she fell in love with the attic room that was originally planned as a bunk room. She laid claim to it because it's quiet and has great views of the lake—and now it's off-limits to family. The window seat near the stone fireplace is Meg's favorite place to curl up and remember seasons past while watching her children down at the lake making their own summertime memories.

There are no counters around the sink, so no time has to be spent clearing away countertop clutter.

In Focus

There isn't a scrap of drywall in Meg's cabin; it's finished inside with salvaged structural rough-sawn wood. To create the weathered interior, aged circular-saw-blade marks were left in the old Douglas fir rafters. For added texture, the walls are constructed using the back of new, locally grown butternut boards.

Meg's away place has a sunny
window seat, a crackling fire,
and a sheltering ceiling.

A former boathouse left in
good shape was found on the
property and renovated into
a cozy 300-sq.-ft. one-room
guest cabin. The family
stayed here during the construction of the new cabin,
which is on the other side
of the pier.

A Family-Size Lakefront Lodge

This lakeside lodge occupies the site of an old general store. The views across the water, the flat beach perfect for bonfires, and the mountains beyond drew one family to this piece of property.

A FAMILY LODGE WAS THE KIND OF PLACE THAT ANN AND DAVID

Danford had in mind for their getaway on the shores of Lake Wenatchee, a

cool, stream-fed body of water in the foothills of the Cascade Mountains of

central Washington. The family was drawn to the area because of the lake-

side scenery and miles of hiking trails that weave throughout the nearby

Wenatchee National Forest and Lake Wenatchee State Park.

David had spent time in Adirondack camps when he lived on the East

Coast and always admired their rustic, relaxed feeling. But the couple

didn't want the oversize spaces that can make a lodge feel like a hotel. They

worked with architect Kevin Kane to design a family lodge and separate

The family takes advantage of nearby recreational activities, such as skiing and mountain-bike riding, but when they are relaxing at the lodge, the lake becomes the focus of their fun. The Nason Ridge Mountains and their reflection in the lake produce a breathtaking view from the dining-room terrace.

Aniline dye brings color into the interior. With less pigment in it than stain, the dye lets the character of wood show through. The dining room table in the foreground was built from a tree cut down when the house was constructed. At the far end, the kitchen tucks under the sitting room loft.

guesthouse for their lakeside property. Here, hidden behind pines off a secluded country road, the family and their guests gather for tranquil vacations. They've grown to enjoy the long drive from Seattle, their heart rates calming as the roads diminish in scale as they approach the lakeside setting.

Open to the Outdoors

The first building a visitor sees is a two-car garage that has guest quarters on the second floor. The building is angled in such a way that it shields the main house from the road. A covered walkway links the garage to the main house beyond.

There are three covered entryways to the 2,300-sq.-ft. main lodge. The formal entry is on the side of the building that faces the road, but almost everyone uses a more casual side entry. A third entry opens out onto a broad terrace that spills down toward the lake.

The lodge's living room, dining room, and kitchen all have views of the lake and feel open to the outdoors. But the living room is also designed with cozy alcoves on both sides of the massive stone fireplace, giving homeowners and guests warm retreats for curling up with

First Floor

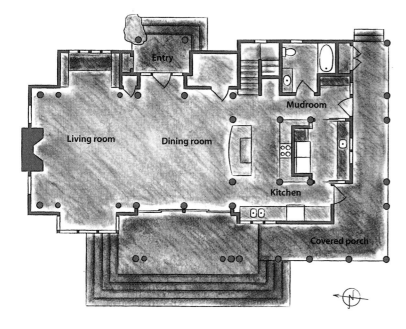

In Focus

These flying creatures won't bother anyone. Laser-cut mosquito and dragonfly motifs illuminate the steel balcony railing overlooking the kitchen. They pay homage to the local insect population.

To make the most of every inch of space, a cookbook nook and seat are carved out of the base of the stairs next to the kitchen.

books, playing board games, or chatting over coffee while looking out into the forest.

There's another snug place upstairs. Behind the balcony that overlooks the living and dining area is a small sitting area, often used as an extra sleeping space. Two bedrooms are tucked behind the sitting area.

When the Danfords aren't relaxing indoors, they're sitting on the terrace looking out at the lake. The water sparkles with light reflected off the snowcapped mountains. The the family's getaway is just two hours from their Seattle home, but the magical views and the serene lodgings make it seem more like a world away.

A barn door slides on an interior track to seal off the kitchen and living room from the bedrooms in the guesthouse. The wall of built-in shelves and cabinets behind the sliding door separates two sleeping berths from one another.

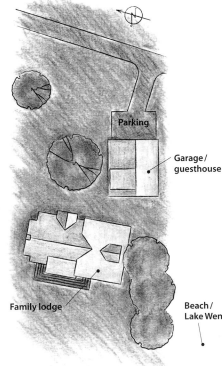

Down to the Lake

Parking

Garage/ guesthouse

Family lodge

Beach/ Lake Wenatchee

The posts create little nooks on both sides of the fireplace where one can pull up a chair or pillow and read next to the window.

Alder saplings, readily available in the area, were used to make a whimsical railing that offers a sense of privacy while letting air and light filter through to the loft space in the guesthouse.

A Simple Design
Deep in the Woods

Two porches flank the cottage's living room. Light bounces off the red-tinged wood walls of the room, casting a golden glow outdoors.

A ONE-MILE HIKE IN THE SNOW DOESN'T DETER A NEW HAMPSHIRE couple from making regular weekend treks to their remote cottage getaway. The first time they saw the 218-acre parcel of land on the Internet, they knew it was where they would find the tranquility they sought. Architect Ward D'Elia designed a simple, 1,200-sq.-ft. timber-frame cottage with fine-crafted woodworking and ironwork details. Whether the couple is snow-shoeing to the cottage under starlit skies with a weekend's worth of supplies strapped to their backs or driving down the rugged gravel road during milder weather, there is nothing more exhilarating to them than catching the first glimpse of their hideaway within the forest of 100-year-old pine and hemlock trees.

This window seat, tucked behind the dining area, receives southern light. The pane pattern expresses a Craftsman-like design.

To honor the site, landscaping around the cottage is kept to a minimum. The stones in the driveway are relocated from elsewhere on the property, and native plants and shrubs found in the woods were transplanted nearer the house.

Finely crafted masonry and creative ironwork give this fieldstone fireplace an unusual character. The wood storage rack made out of iron is designed to look like an antique sleigh and the mantelpiece is a contrasting Douglas fir. Metal pulls on the fireplace screen are angled to echo the shape of an oversize triangular stone on the fireplace surround.

Minding the Landscape

The homeowners treasure their property's pristine qualities. The land is part of an ongoing 600-acre conservation initiative that includes frontage along two ponds. The owners negotiated an arrangement to build their getaway on the shores of one pond, where a few cabins had already been built, in exchange for leaving their property along the other pond undeveloped.

The desire to blend in with the wooded environment drove the understated design of this efficient but charming Timberpeg®-framed cottage. Few trees were felled for its construction. The house is not visible from the pond, but careful tree trimming allows the homeowners to catch sight of the shimmering water from inside the cottage.

A lift in the roof provided enough room for the addition of transom windows. The upper sashes on the side broaden the panoramic view from the living room out to the forest and the pond below.

The entrance to the cottage has a ramp designed to bridge a drainage swale. It can also be used for handicap access.

Few walls interrupt the flow of space inside the cottage. The kitchen is open to both the informal dining area and the screened porch that overlooks the pond. The doors to the screened porch open outward rather than in—a small detail, but nevertheless an important one that conserves limited interior space.

Conserving Space

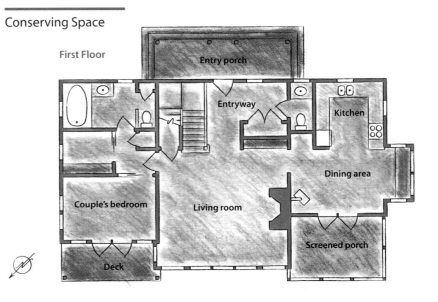

First Floor

Entry porch

Entryway

Kitchen

Couple's bedroom

Living room

Dining area

Deck

Screened porch

The structural timber framing on the screened porch is shaped to mimic the arching limbs of the trees in the forest.

Deep in the Woods

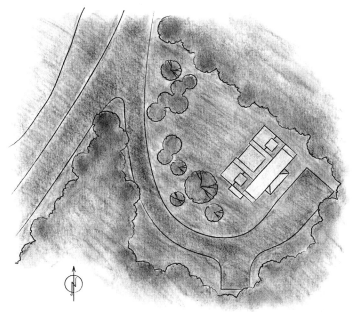

A Well-Detailed Cottage

Despite its simple floor plan, the house has a distinct sense of charm and craftsmanship that's derived from the woodworking, ironwork, and masonry details both inside and out.

Outside, the underside of the cottage was exposed since it was built on stilts, but wood trellis trim hides the base while adding a richly textured detail to the cedar-shingle façade. The exterior window trim of black anodized metal outlines the windows against the warm wood and brings added quality and depth to the openings. Even the brackets—indoors and out—provide lateral bracing that's both decorative and structural. All elements add to the cottage's enchanting character.

LIVING WITHIN THE LAW Building in an area that's protected by a conservation easement is a lesson in balancing the interests of those who want to enjoy the serenity of the land with those who want to live on it. A conservation easement is a legal agreement with a local land trust or government agency that limits the amount and type of development that can take place, all the while leaving the land in private ownership. (The land can be sold or passed down to heirs with the same developmental restrictions.) It's a voluntary land-protection tool, privately initiated by homeowners, and its primary purpose is to conserve natural and man-made resources on the land. The beauty of a conservation easement is that it stops commercial construction and residential subdivisions from taking over the land, a desirable agreement for homeowners of private getaways such as this one.

Books are an essential ingredient for the getaway experience. Here, they are stored behind glass for easy selection and minimal dust collection.

Planned for Weekend Use

The cottage is designed specifically for weekend visits, which means the floor plan is simple and straightforward without any formal spaces. That way, there's no fuss or muss when homeowners and guests hurry in and out of the cottage while carrying luggage and recreational gear.

Adding to the informality is an open floor plan designed without hallways. Downstairs, the living room separates the couple's bedroom suite from the kitchen and dining room, so the homeowners can sleep late while guests clatter in the kitchen making breakfast. Upstairs, a loftlike study serves as a transition area between two bedrooms.

Keeping things simple and protecting the land have paid off for the homeowners. Their surroundings offer the possibility for magical encounters. The homeowners have seen a pair of owls eavesdropping outside the cabin while the radio played. And one winter day a moose sauntered up to a window, surprising one of the owners who was curled up in the window seat engrossed in a good book.

The countertops and tub surround in the main-floor bathroom are made with granite mined from quarries in Deer Isle, Maine. The stone contrasts with the warm colors of the cherry wood cabinets and Douglas fir framing.

Upstairs, two bedrooms flank a study that overlooks the living areas. Light from skylights and a pair of windows reaches the first floor living areas.

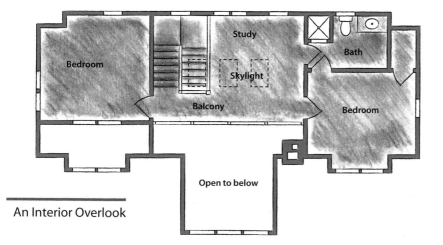

Bedroom

Study

Bath

Skylight

Balcony

Bedroom

Open to below

An Interior Overlook

An Accessible Getaway

This accessible getaway sits gracefully in the Vermont landscape. On the outside, its weathered shingles create an ambience of an old New England summer camp.

SUMMERHOUSES ARE OFTEN COMPACT WITH NARROW DOORWAYS, cramped bathrooms, and steep stairways. So when a retired couple from Washington, D.C., bought some land with an old cabin near a tranquil Vermont lake, they acknowledged that the house had the same problem they encountered many times with summer rentals. The cabin was not wheelchair accessible.

Rather than trying to adapt the existing cabin, they started from scratch. Architect Patrick Kane designed a simple summer home that is accessible without compromising style and charm. The 1,800-sq.-ft. house is contemporary and spacious, with a ramp to the front door that enables the homeowners to move freely about and enjoy the outdoors.

The Scandinavian simplicity of this getaway is defined by bright, well-lit rooms and natural cedar walls with exposed wood rafters. The living spaces all flow comfortably from one room to the next with easy wheelchair access.

To keep the space clutter free for maximum wheelchair movement, there's minimal free-standing furniture in the living room. The couch and bookcases are built in so they don't protrude far into the living space.

A **Simple**, Single Level

From the road, the one-level house looks like two small weathered shingle-style cottages connected by a breezeway. Up close, it's evident that the house is L-shaped, with a wheelchair ramp that is inconspicuous even though it rises from the parking pad to a covered deck and finally to the front door. The top of the ramp is flush with the deck to create a seamless transition.

The deck is more like a courtyard or a front porch. The homeowners can sit here in privacy, enjoying the view, but they're also in the right place to meet and greet visitors when they arrive.

The deck leads indoors to a vestibule. Though it looks like a breezeway from afar, it's really the entry hall that divides the house into two sections. One side is the couple's bedroom and the other has the living area and kitchen.

The large floor-to-ceiling window in the living room makes the space feel as though it extends into the outdoor setting. The window's height enables anyone to enjoy nature without going outside, whether they are standing up or sitting down in a wheelchair.

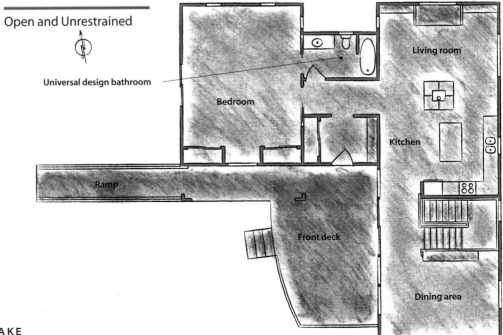

Open and Unrestrained

Universal design bathroom

Living room

Bedroom

Kitchen

Ramp

Front deck

Dining area

Three small windows let in light and preserve some privacy in the bedroom, which faces the front of the house. Larger windows overlook the backyard.

The open cabinets make kitchenware easy to find and accessible. The metal tie rods hold the roof in place while giving an open, spacious feeling to the cabin.

IN FOCUS

The wheelchair ramp is crafted so that it looks like a natural extension of the house. Its gentle, shallow slope hugs the landscape so it seems like a path to the house that just happens to ramped. And matching materials help accessible forms blend in with the surroundings.

At Home among the Trees

The forest setting inspired the choice of materials used inside the house. Heartwood pine floors, knotty pine wainscoting, and a field-stone fireplace create a traditional but luminous cottage interior.

A

FTER KEVIN BOLAND BOUGHT AN ACRE OF LAKESIDE PROPERTY
in northern Michigan, he and his wife, Marilyn, camped there for more than a decade, setting aside money, gathering ideas for a cottage, and enjoying the smell of fallen pine needles. By the time the couple was ready to start building a getaway home, they had developed a strong connection to the pines that tower over the property.

In deference to those trees, they built a 2½-story cottage that emerges from the woodland like a pine tree itself. Architect Marco Silveri designed the structure with the smallest footprint possible to minimize the number of trees that would have to be cut down. With its tall, slender shape and steeply pitched roof, the house blends in perfectly with the forest that surrounds it.

Except for a small path down to the water, most of the shoreline was left shrouded in natural vegetation.

To cultivate the feeling that this cottage has been here a long time and that the ground was never disturbed, several inches of pine needles were raked and stored before construction and then redistributed when the project was finished. Shingle and clapboard siding stained an earthy taupe blends with the encircling trees.

Standing Tall

The Bolands were drawn to the property, which is four hours north of their home in Detroit, because it is in a woodsy, recreational area. The cottage's tall, rectangular form doesn't take up much space on the ground. The rooms are stacked in three levels, giving the top two floors spectacular views in all directions.

The cottage is surrounded by trees, some almost within arm's reach out the second floor-windows. The third-floor guest area and billiard room is the place where visitors can gaze out over the treetops at the harvest moon. The couple refers to their three-story cottage as a tree house since it reaches high up into the leaves. But its presence complements the surrounding forest.

A Compact Cottage

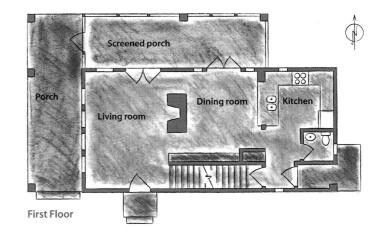

First Floor

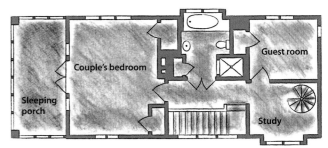

Second Floor

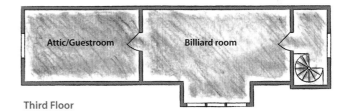

Third Floor

The use of natural materials, such as slab stone stairs, diminishes the presence of a modern structure in the landscape.

The second-floor sleeping porch in this lakeside cottage offers the home-owners a way to surround themselves with the sights and sounds of their forested property. It has three different views out to the lake and into the woods.

The cool air moves through the sleeping porch at night, making the couple feel as if they were sleeping outdoors.

Porchside Oasis

The couple's second-floor bedroom suite is a retreat that includes a breeze-filled sleeping porch overlooking the lake. It's accessible only through their room. On this porch, they watch the sunset or sleep while listening to the calls of the whippoorwill. The second-floor bathroom has its own lake views through a large window over the bathtub. A small guest room is also on this level.

Informality Encouraged

One section of the covered wraparound porch is open and the other part screened to give homeowners and guests places to relax whatever the weather. Both parts

A CONTEMPORARY COTTAGE The Bolands wanted their lake home to have a traditional, rustic character but with a light feel and modern touches throughout. Brightening up the rooms was especially important in this cottage since a deep porch wraps around two sides of the house. All of the wood in the interior is light-colored pine finished with a clear varnish. Wood trim is finished with a coat of clear, water-based ure-thane rather than an oil-based product, which would darken over time. The cottage's modern touches are evident in the oversize panes of glass in the French doors that lead out to the porch.

A spiral staircase leads to the third-floor attic and game room. Nestled under the roof, the attic space is the place for a game of billiards when the weather keeps guests indoors.

A south-facing porch is usually desirable in forest settings because it will get more sunlight. But because the south side of this house is in the forest's understory, both porches were placed on the north side of the cottage. As a bonus, scenery viewed in northern sun appears sharp and clear.

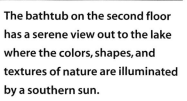

The bathtub on the second floor has a serene view out to the lake where the colors, shapes, and textures of nature are illuminated by a southern sun.

An open porch has advantages that make up for the lack of enclosure. It provides a place for outdoor cooking and storage of frequently used gear.

Most of the couple's shoreline property remains wooded for privacy, but they selectively opened some views, including an area around the dock.

of the porch have sweeping views of the lake. The porch becomes part mudroom when homeowners and guests drop off the hiking boots, beach clothes, and fishing poles they used down by the lake.

The 8-ft.-deep porch offers a choice of spaces for relaxation, each capturing a different view of the site. After a day of activities, there's nothing more rejuvenating than sitting down on the porch, inhaling the fresh fragrances of the forest, and taking in an all-embracing view of the lake.

Tall and Slender above the Lake

Architects and Designers

On The Plains and In The Hills

A Dog Trot in the Woods *(pp. 16–23)*
Mitch Blake, AIA
Ward and Blake Architects
200 East Broadway
P.O. Box 10399
Jackson, WY 83002
(307) 733-6897
www.wardblakearchitects.com

Little Hamlet on the Prairie
(pp. 24–31)
Candace Tillotson Miller, AIA
P.O. Box 470
208 West Park Street
Livingston, MT 59047
(406) 222-7057
www.ctmarchitects.com

A Screened House in Hill Country
(pp. 32–37)
William Barbee, AIA
Barbee Architects, Inc.
2116 Hancock Drive
Austin, TX 78756
(512) 323-2116
www.barbeeinc.com

Reclaiming a Farmstead
(pp. 38–45)
Laura Hartman, AIA
Fernau & Hartman Architects, Inc.
2512 Ninth Street, # 2
Berkeley, CA 94710
(510) 848-4480
www.fernauhartman.com

A New Camp Compound
(pp. 46–53)
Rob Whitten, AIA
Whitten Architects
37 Silver Street
P.O. Box 404
Portland, ME 04112
(207) 774-0111
www.whittenarchitects.com

A Villa in the Hills *(pp. 54–61)*
David Arkin, AIA
Arkin Tilt Architects
1101 8th Street, #180
Berkeley, CA 94710
(510) 528-9830
www.arkintilt.com

Along The Coast

A Farmhouse by the Sea
(pp. 64–69)
James Estes, AIA
Estes/Twombly Architects, Inc.
79 Thames Street
Newport, RI 02840
(401) 846-3336
www.estestwombly.com

A Shed under the Stars
(pp. 70–75)
Brian MacKay-Lyons, FAIA
Brian MacKay-Lyons Architect, Ltd.
2188 Gottingen Street
Halifax, Nova Scotia, Canada B3K3B4
(902) 429-1867
www.bmlaud.ca

Simplicity above the Dunes
(pp. 90–95)
Preston T. Phillips, Architect
P.O. Box 3037
Bridgehampton, NY 11932
(631) 537-1237
www.prestontphillips.com

A Cabin with a Story *(pp. 108–115)*
Jay Dalgliesh, AIA
Dalgliesh, Eichman, Gilpin and Paxton
Architects
206 5th Street, Northeast
Charlottesville, VA 22902
(804) 977-4480

A Plantation on a Waterway
(pp. 76–83)
Dale Mulfinger, FAIA
SALA Architects, Inc.
440 2nd Street
Excelsior, MN 55331
(952) 380-4817
www.SALAarc.co

A Neighborhood with Ocean Views
(pp. 96–99)
Tom Thacher, AIA
Thacher and Thompson Architects
200 Washington St., #201
Santa Cruz, CA 95060
(831) 457-3939
www.tntarch.com

A House in the Sun *(pp. 116–123)*
John Barton, AIA
Casa Mirasol
P.O. Box 195
Ojo Caliente, NM 87549
(505) 583-2429
www.jwbarton.com

A Wilderness Perch with Harbor Views
(pp. 84–89)
David Vandervort, AIA
David Vandervort Architects
5135 Ballard Avenue Northwest
Seattle, WA 98107
(206) 784-1614
www.vandervort.com

In The Mountains

A Modern Barn on the Mountianside
(pp. 102–107)
Harry Teague, AIA
Harry Teague Architects
412 North Mill Street
Aspen, CO 81611
(970) 925-2556
www.harryteaguearchitects.com

Building a Family Legacy *(pp. 124–131)*
Katherine Hillbrand, AIA
SALA Architects, Inc.
904 South 4th Street
Stillwater, MN 55082
(651) 351-0961
www.SALAarc.com

A Bit of Italy *(pp. 132–139)*
Elizabeth Reader, AIA, and Charles Swartz, AIA
The Kurtz Building
2 North Cameron Street
Winchester, VA 22601
(540) 665-0212
www.readerswartz.com

A Submerged Ski House in the Snow *(pp. 140–145)*
Mark Horton, AIA
Mark Horton Architecture
101 South Park
San Francisco, CA 94107
(415) 543-3347
www.mh-a.com

BY THE LAKE

Celebrating the Forces of Nature *(pp. 148–151)*
Dale Mulfinger, FAIA
SALA Architects, Inc.
440 2nd Street
Excelsior, MN 55331
(952) 380-4817
www.SALAarc.com

A New Porch Cabin *(pp. 152–157)*
Dale Mulfinger, FAIA
SALA Architects, Inc.
440 2nd Street
Excelsior, MN 55331
(952) 380-4817
www.SALAarc.com

A Family-Size Lakefront Lodge *(pp. 158–163)*
Kevin Kane
Snyder, Hartung, Kane and Strauss Architects
1050 North 38th Street
Seattle, WA 98103
(206) 675-9151
www.shksarchitects.com

A Simple Design Deep in the Woods *(pp. 164–171)*
Ward D'Elia, AIA
Samyn-D'Elia Architects, P. A.
P.O. Box 1259
Ashland, NH 03217
(603) 968-7133
www.sdarchitects.com

An Accessible Getaway *(pp. 172–175)*
Patrick Kane, Architect, formerly with:
Black River Design, Architects
73 Main Street, Room #9
Montpelier, VT 05602
(802) 223-2044
www.blackriverdesign.com

At Home among the Trees *(pp. 176–183)*
Marco Silveri, AIA
Silveri Architects
650 Livernois
Ferndale, MI 48220
(248) 591-0360
www.silveri.com